To Joe and Hari

You can be anything you want to
be in your life if you have
inspiration, determination, motivation
and a little bit of luck!

Work hard, play hard, and
never give up!

Nigel Kennerly
June 21st 2012.

PRIDE, PEDALS
AND PAIN

PRIDE, PEDALS AND PAIN

Nigel Cleevely

CGE Publishing Ltd.

First published in Great Britain by CGE Publishing Ltd.

ISBN 978-1-909061-03-3

Printed and bound by Good News Books, Ongar, Essex.

This book is dedicated to my wife, Christine,
and children, Daniel, James, Charlotte and Thomas,
for their support, encouragement and threats!

Foreword

This is a book about a man approaching 65 years of age who has never been able to resist a challenge. After knowing him for almost 50 years I can vouch for that!

After Brian Clough rejected him as a professional footballer at just 22 years of age, indirectly enabling Derby County to go on and win the Division 1 Championship, he fought his way to the top of the travel industry before settling for a peaceful life in the Cotswolds Hills.

However, retirement presents its own challenges; overcoming boredom being one of them and when most people were seeking out 'pipe and slippers' he began plotting one final adventure – to ride solo on a bicycle from Land's End to John O'Groats. It would be the first time he had sat on a bike since the age of 16.

Why did he take on the ride? Partly to get fit but predominantly to serve as an example to his children or anyone, that just about anything could be achieved if the body was physically sound and the mind strong and disciplined.

This epic story begins six months before his departure and details his complete training schedule, his route planning preparation, not to mention his first minor task of discarding over 40 lb of unwanted fat!

His ride, written in a very 'tongue in cheek' style, highlights precise details of his journey north, a fascinating brief history of the towns he rode through, the fierce climatic changes he endured besides constant recollections of the many unique characters he met en route, me being one of them. Equally as important he provides fascinating feedback on his physical and mental well-being as he rode almost 1100 miles through the country lanes and A roads of England, Wales and Scotland.

A wonderful insight into a marathon solo cycle ride by a man who simply refused to lie down. I think Brian Clough would have been impressed.

Alan Durban
Derby County and Wales

Acknowledgements

To all the sponsors who gave so generously to the Derby County Former Players' Charity for 2010, the Derbyshire Children's Holiday Centre. Also to the television progammes Escape to the Country and The Weakest Link for getting me through the hours spent on the static bike.

Finally, to Nigel Methley and Adrian Tremlett for their encouragement and motivational powers. Without their recommendation I would not have experienced The Crask Inn.

Contents

Introduction

WHAT drives people to seek adventure, pitting themselves against the power of oceans, the perils of mountains, deserts and jungles?

What is it that motivates individuals to climb, swim, run, cycle or trek further or higher than anyone before them? Putting it bluntly, why the hell do they do it?

Nobody has been able to give me a credible answer. But many do and record books and adventure stories proliferate with examples of those who have taken on both the might of nature and physical endurance and gained fame if not fortune.

In recent times TV presenter Ben Fogle and Olympian James Cracknell have rowed the Atlantic and Ranulph Fiennes, at the ripe old age of 59, has run seven marathons in seven days on seven different continents, just four months after undergoing a double heart bypass operation.

Why, even the once rotund and much loved Eddie Izzard, at the tender age of 47, managed what sounded like the impossible: to run an incredible 43 marathons in just 51 days.

Even my younger brother, Adrian, had got himself in on the act by driving, pitching and putting himself into the Guinness Book of Records, playing 18 holes of golf on six different courses on six consecutive days. Not particularly difficult you may think – until I tell you that the golf courses were as far apart as Cairo, Singapore, Melbourne, Santiago, Miami and the Isle of Man. Yes, a round of golf on every continent around the world in just six days.

Never mind the more famous names that had gone before, even my baby brother had eclipsed me in the adventure stakes.

It's not that the thought of adventure was in any way alien to me, for I'd had my fair share in my 63 years on Planet Earth. When I was 18, I left my native Cheltenham and moved the 100 miles north to Derby to become a professional footballer with Derby County.

I'd played with and against some of the great names of the 1960s, trodden the hallowed turf of Old Trafford, Anfield, Molineux and Villa Park to name but a few. I had even toured with the Rams in Czechoslovakia, East Germany and Bulgaria.

After moving into the semi-professional football wilderness with Burton Albion – like a few others, I didn't survive Brian Clough at Derby – I went on to enjoy a very successful career in the tourism industry, travelling the world while still finding the time and energy to run a few marathons, my best time being in Paris when I completed the 26-plus miles in a shade over three hours.

I'd also aimed high and climbed the three peaks of Snowdon, Scafell and Ben Nevis in the space of two muscle-aching days.

After that, hiking the length of the Pennine and Cotswold Ways were walks in the park, even if the parks did contain knee-deep peat bogs and steep climbs.

But in honesty those little escapades were no real great shakes for a man in his thirties crammed full of energy, vitality and desire, plus a fair sprinkling of vanity and conceit. All of those I had in abundance as I chalked off macho mini ambitions, mere stepping-stones to justify yet more celebratory beers and nights away with the lads.

But hard facts now had to be faced, times had changed. Gone was the svelte figure bounding with energy and drive, replaced by a man, retired for nine years, whose idea of strenuous exercise was walking slowly round a golf course – if the weather conditions were perfect.

Not only that, the aforementioned well-honed athlete had metamorphosed into a shape resembling a barrel, a barrel that weighed a massive 14 st 10 lb. OK if you are 6 ft 6 in tall, but not too clever if you stand barely 5 ft 8 in.

Checking the Body Mass Index chart (BMI) only made it worse, as it stated clearly that I was officially obese and by some distance. I didn't dwell on the computer screen too long, for there was no guarantee that 'obese' wasn't prefaced by the word 'extremely!'

Can you imagine the scene when I returned to Derby to attend the former players' annual dinner or summer golf day? I was no longer the 9 st 7 lb Football League winger with a fair turn of speed; more like a short roly-poly Sunday League stopper with a fair girth of fat.

Anyone who has played sport will know that dressing rooms full of athletes are perfect breeding grounds for banter and mickey-taking and I was a sitting target. There was no place to run – too slow. And no place to hide – too fat. I just had to smile and take it.

My only pathetic excuse for my shape was that for the last 30 years I had been helping the Chilean, Australian and South African Governments get their red wine export industries up and running. While it had greatly improved each country's economy, it had taken a heavy toll on my body shape, not to mention my pocket.

So, to return to the question: 'Why do people seek adventure and pit themselves against the might of the natural world?' On a personal basis, one reason was more than clear: to lose 40 lb of unwanted fat and stop the continuous ridicule from my football peers Roy McFarland, Colin Boulton and Alan Durban.

But there were more reasons, other than weight-related ones, that willed me to get off my backside and do something. I wanted to set my four children an example, to show them that just about anything can be achieved in life with the right mental and physical application.

At the same time I wanted to regain a bit of the respect that I had lost due to being continually caught slumped semi-comatose in my favourite chair watching Sky Sports channels along with my close friends, Merlot and Shiraz.

But, deep down, I was motivated to seek adventure, to actually achieve a feat that would require a great deal of effort and discipline. I wanted to do it for me, to convince myself that I still had a bit of fight in me, even if I was past my peak.

In brief I needed an adventure that would restore my self-esteem and personal pride.

Ironically I found the motivation and inspiration while slumped in front of the TV, watching sport. There they were, riding in the 2009 Tour de France, Bradley Wiggins and Mark Cavendish. Two Britons, showing the world what could be achieved when a massive amount of guts and stamina were applied. Perfect examples of athletes that had reached super fitness levels by hard graft.

Immediately I knew what I wanted to do.

At the age of 64 years and 5 months I would ride solo from Land's End to John O'Groats, via 'B' roads and country lanes - a distance of over 1,000 miles.

Now where should I begin?

Some Training Tips

GETTING back on a bike on a daily basis after a barren period of over 50 years was quite an education. Suppleness, agility and balance that are taken as the norm in mid-teens had long departed, replaced by a vulnerability honed from many years spent sitting comfortably in the warmth and safety of a modern saloon car.

Regardless of my initial discomfort, my preparation had to begin if I was to ride the length of Great Britain. Losing the equivalent of a five year old child's weight and building up sufficient stamina to ride 70 miles every day for a fortnight, had to commence and be maintained.

Metaphorically speaking, the show had to get on the road.

For the greater part of November, December, January and February my training rides were restricted to my static bike in front of the television – *Escape to the Country* and *The Weakest Link* being my training partners as I fought the flab and built up stamina.

With only the occasional day off, I endeavoured to ride for at least an hour every day, burning around 850 calories a time as I aimed to bring my weight down from 14 st 10 lb to 12 st 13 lb in just four months. Then a further 14 lb between March and the end of May.

It would be wrong of me to say it was easy because it wasn't – anything but. Not only was I paralysing my mind by sitting astride an exercise bike going nowhere, I was also forcing myself to endure a pasta-driven, fat-free diet with only minimal alcohol intake on two days of the week.

Many is the Monday that I have awoken and jumped on the scales to see that a weekend with a few beers and glasses of wine have put my weight reduction back by a week. It really was a case of two steps forward and one step back – with too many times taking one forward and two back.

I had scheduled February to be the month when I really hit the road, but, as you will shortly read, those plans were soon just 'pie in the sky'– it would be a further month before I could regularly ride with the breeze on my face, the Cotswold countryside replacing the Sony TV.

There can be no doubt that, without my static bike training in the long dark, cold and wet months of winter, I could never have embarked on the six-month training programme that I had set myself in order to prepare my body for the 'End-to-End' challenge. In retrospect it was the perfect preparation prior to my final three months on the road before my ride.

In March, I was able to get out on my road bike on 18 days, covering a distance of 471 miles, an average of 26 miles a day. Add an additional seven hours of riding indoors and I was beginning to feel as though progress was being made. Even though I only lost 4 lb during the month, I was within half a stone of my goal weight and still had two months of training before I was scheduled to leave Land's End.

During the month of April, I trained 25 times, all but one on the road, covering a distance just short of 700 miles and averaging 29 miles a day – a huge improvement on the previous month. With a further 4 lb disappearing, I was only 3 lb away from my target.

Even with my training in the final week of May tailing off, I still managed to clock up 571 miles in the 22 days of riding the roads, maintaining an average of 26 miles per day. With another couple of pounds lost I was very close to my 12 st target weight I had set myself – in seven months a loss of 40 lb. To fully realize the enormity of that, pop into your local supermarket and pick up 18 1 kg bags of sugar – that's the weight that I had shed.

No wonder I was feeling smug and confident enough to write a few tongue-in-cheek words of advice for budding long-distance cyclists – having said that, they may not be too far from the truth.

Here are the thoughts of a complete novice to the world of cycling on how to counter the problems of aching muscles, overgrown gardens and fellow citizens on the road. You never know – they may help.

AVOID HORTICULTURE

When training, don't be tempted to enviously gaze at people who are working in their gardens. Yes, I do understand that your patch is an embarrassment due to the time you are spending in the saddle and I do appreciate that your lawn needs scarifying at least four times to rake out the winter moss.

Believe me, I really am sympathetic that it is now mid-May and you still have to fertilize, mow, or edge. Don't fret. An old auntie of mine firmly holds the belief that ants, moles, leather jackets, crows and even muntjacs always make a beeline for freshly manicured greensward. She is adamant that anyone messing with nature deserves to be punished.

Ride on by while smiling knowingly at the green–fingered simpletons, knowing that their fate is out of their hands.

STRETCH

Find time to stretch at least six times a day with particular emphasis on your thigh muscles. Each session will only take a minute and reward you a hundredfold.

Here's how you do it:

With one hand firmly holding a stationary object – the wife or a chair back are two useful suggestions – use the other hand to grasp the front of your ankle and pull your leg up behind you to stretch the thigh.

Count slowly to 20, and then repeat using the other leg. Never attempt to save time by doing both legs at the same time – you won't feel the benefit. In an emergency you can complete this exercise when cycling – but here is another little piece of advice: make sure you are travelling downhill as inclines can prove to be tricky.

VEHICLES

Many times during your ride you will feel tired and emotional and feel that the world is against you. You will look for someone or something to blame for your plight.

Vehicles and their drivers will be an easy target, but take my advice: just think nasty thoughts; do refrain from gesticulating or shouting abuse at them.

It's not easy I know, but stay strong – they have as much right on the road as you and mean you no harm. If you do weaken and want to vent your irritability and frustration on them, follow my guidelines.

In simple terms, choose your target very carefully as some are more dangerous than others. Here is my handy guide to potential victims.

VERY HIGH RISK – HGV DRIVERS

Easily spotted as they drive extremely large vehicles and will be sporting a shaven head, t–shirt with an egg-stained front and jeans at least four inches below health and safety guidelines on a long departed waist.

They will also be heavily tattooed, but don't be fooled by the 'I love Mum' on the right forearm or the rather contradictory Arabic inscription on the other that translates to 'Jesus is Great'. Even Captains of HGVs have moments of weakness.

They can also lip read, even through a mud stained wing mirror. The great majority are not afraid to stop either, and after carefully helping you down from your bike will demand that you repeat your utterances straight to their unshaven faces. Don't be surprised if they expel a series of expletives very rarely heard south of Watford.

Basically, when this happens you have two choices. One, pretend that you are foreign, hunch your shoulders and with palms facing upwards jabber away in gobbledygook. Alternatively, drop to your knees, grab him round one leg, sob loudly and beg for mercy. In extreme circumstances do both. One final piece of advice – practise, practise, practise, it's time well spent.

HIGH RISK – WHITE VAN DRIVERS

This species is not dangerous and will only rarely stop to confront you.

Their prime aim in life is to get their deliveries completed as soon as humanly possible and be in the bookies before the 2.15 race from Kempton is out of the stalls. Besides, their eyes are only infrequently on the road as they have *The Sun* to read between drops, as well as last night's kebab to finish. However, remember, they are frustrated, failed HGV drivers and carry a grudge. They can turn nasty, not by leaving their warm cab, but by resorting to hand gestures of defiance. A cupped hand moving from left to right for male cyclists and a middle finger heading northwards for female cyclists is their idea of adult wit.

If they perform both to you do not be dismayed or seek medical advice, they failed their HGV exam due to poor eyesight.

Generally it is best to ignore them. Not like the cyclist I once read about. He carried on a running battle with a WVD for over three miles in Merseyside, utilising both hand and mouth profanities while travelling at a speed well in excess of 15 mph. He was getting the upper hand until they turned a corner and found the traffic in front at a standstill.

I must admit I lost a bit of respect for him when I read on and learned that he turned his bike round and rode back in the direction he had come from – not stopping or looking back until he was just outside Chester.

Not just cowardly but very time consuming.

MEDIUM RISK – CARAVANS

Normally caravans are not a problem as the car, or more accurately the 4x4, will be driven by a man well over the age of 55 who will almost always have, what old-timers call, a 'dickie hip'. With restricted mobility he can easily be outrun.

But here's a tip: stay on guard. A friend of mine was once having a mild contretemps with the driver of a caravan when, out of the side door of their home on wheels appeared a stone-faced harridan waving a metal spatula. Leaping from the van she proceeded to chase him for several hundred yards before slowing to a halt shouting her final volley of abuse.

My friend reckons she probably served her teenage years as a cashier on the dodgems at the fair and couldn't get it out of her system.

LOW RISK – OPEN TOP SPORTS CARS

Unlikely to be seen, except in Cornwall or around the Glenshee area. If a male drives the car, the upper thighs of his female companion will invariably preoccupy him. If travelling alone, his recently purchased top of the range sat nav will be craving his attention.

My advice on this one is – take nothing for granted, have a plan. Let me help you on this one. If he leaves his car and wanders over, there are three areas that you can exploit.

First pull his cap, or more probably his deerstalker, down over his eyes.

Second, holding his white silk scarf firmly with two hands, tighten, twist and pull skywards.

And finally – and this is the difficult bit – yank his leather gloves off his hands and store safely. Their sheepskin-lined, string-backed, haberdashery will prove a godsend for you when in the Highlands.

But don't overdo it. If he squeals: 'Mummy, he is hurting me' – then the show is over; let him go and continue on your way, not forgetting the gloves.

You've had your fun and there are still miles to cover.

LOW RISK – WOMEN DRIVERS

They won't see you.

One Eye On Spain

WITH England still in the depths of winter and me sick to death of my static indoor exercise bike I decided to seek refuge in one of the homes of cycling – Spain. The warm weather would do me good and the change of scene would refresh my mind.

When I flew from Birmingham, one Friday in late January, life was feeling good. My destination was my apartment at Oliva Nova midway between Valencia and Alicante and the opportunity to enjoy five days' cycling in the winter sunshine.

Christine, my wife, was heading to the frozen north – well, Blackpool actually – for a dance convention, so it was sensible that I should put my freedom to good use. It seemed pretty fair to me: one of us fox trotting up the ice-bound M6 while the other was quickstepping along the perfect cycling roads of the Costa Blanca.

I'd earned my short break – three months of daily grind on the indoor exercise bike and the loss of 24 unwanted pounds had conditioned me sufficiently to test myself on a few 50 km 'back-to-back' explorations in the beautiful, mountainous countryside that has housed many stages of the Tour of Spain.

In addition, if it was good enough to regularly host the large number of professional teams that trained in the region's micro-climate, it was good enough for me. Perfect weather, perfect roads - what could possibly go wrong?

Arriving at Alicante airport I took the motorway 100 km north to Parcent, a sleepy village in the Jalon Valley and home to Lyn and Tony, old friends of mine, who six years previously had headed to their permanent place in the sun from our Cotswold village.

Tony had graciously offered to lend me his ageing Peugeot cycle and had even been burning the midnight oil, servicing it for me. Although he was comfortably seven inches taller than me, with the saddle lowered to the frame it would suit me fine. Besides, it would be rude to refuse and more expensive.

After enjoying a pleasant lunch and catching up on life in general, the cycle was reverently stored in my hire car for the 25-minute journey to my apartment at Oliva Nova.

Then, in the space of just 10 seconds, a personal catastrophe struck, a catastrophe that eliminated my plans for cycle training Spanish style and, worse still, put in grave doubts any thoughts I had of riding the minor roads and lanes between Land's End and John O'Groats in May.

In the blink of an eye, literally, my meticulous route planning, the booking of B&B accommodation, the purchasing of ancillary cycling equipment, the loss of weight and the disciplined training all appeared to be a monumental waste of time and effort, not to mention money.

The reason? Not illness as such, not even a muscle twitch, certainly not a sudden lack of motivation. I simply went totally blind in my right eye.

Two weeks prior to my trip, I'd experienced posterior vitreous detachments, more commonly known as floaters, in the eye, and – as I had now found out – it was likely that the flight had irritated the condition which had developed into a vitreous haemorrhage; or put another way, bleeding behind the eye.

My optician in Chipping Norton had already warned me that one in seven people with this ailment develop sight-threatening detached retinas, but in my upbeat state of mind I had been confident I would be in the other group of six. Now, only four hours after disembarking from my flight, I was paying dearly for my optimism.

There was nothing else to do but drive myself to the ultra-modern hospital in Denia to seek advice. After a three-hour wait – don't knock the NHS every time – a very short-tempered specialist appeared.

Before we could get down to business, he insisted that, as we were in his country, I should speak to him in my best Spanish. I failed to understand how reciting the names of five Real Madrid footballers followed by '*hola*' and '*café con leche*' (this being my personal lexicon of his native tongue) would help him reach a diagnosis, but eventually we called a truce and he instructed me to drive to my apartment, lie face down for two days, then report back to him after the weekend.

Clearly the prospect of a one-eyed Englishman driving on pitch-black rush-hour roads in a hire car did not seem to bother him. All good for business I suppose.

I left the hospital even more depressed than when I'd entered, reflecting on my initial error of insisting on an urgent consultation and thus disturbing someone who'd quite likely been sitting at home watching the latest episode of whatever masquerades as the Iberian equivalent of *EastEnders*, when his evening was spoiled.

Lesson one: Don't argue with hospital professionals when they ask you to speak in Spanish – the words Ronaldo, Kaka, Alonso and Raul will have to do; after all, the penalty for failing to comply is two days solitary with your head face-down in a pillow.

The return visit on Monday failed to live up to Friday's excitement, except to confirm my long-held view that the Spanish population speak louder and longer than any other nationality I know.

Not only were waiting patients giving it some verbal, so were all the relatives, including the children, all no doubt enjoying their annual break at the infirmary. Even Spanish kids must get bored with Benidorm after 100 visits.

I felt so alone.

Wednesday was set for my operation, so I had two more days to carefully eye-up – with my good eye, of course – the creased pillow in my bedroom, the boredom eased only by a bottle-bank full of eye drops that I had been prescribed.

Aiming small droplets of liquid into my eye every four hours was fast becoming the highlight of my day.

The operation went well, especially considering the volume of noise in the operating theatre. Throughout the entire procedure I remained awake, the local anaesthetist only injecting a couple of needles above and below the problem eye.

Let me give you some words of advice here. When six Spaniards with large lungs enter into a medical exchange in an operating theatre, sit up and ask for a general anaesthetic. Be warned though, even that may not be enough. Let's just say it was noisy.

Looking like Pudsey Bear, I eventually left the hospital with instructions to return the next day for another examination. Following that were final commands to come back in a week's time for further checks.

Boy, was I suffering for the tetchiness of the specialist I had seen on my first visit. Not only was I now sentenced to spending at least a week longer than I'd planned in my newly adopted country, I wasn't allowed to ride or do anything strenuous.

The bike remained on the back seat of my car, a constant reminder, taunting me every time I went for a drive. It was now 12 days after I had first arrived in Spain and I was still as close to riding a bike as a one-legged man was to winning an arse-kicking competition.

Regardless of the advice from my optical guardians that I should not go anywhere near a bike, I was determined to get in the saddle and at least be able to tell friends that I had done some brief conditioning work in the winter sunshine.

So, within three days of the operation the bike was removed from the car boot and I was off and running albeit for only 10 miles. I was back 45 minutes later, quietly pleased with myself that I had at least in some small way, pedalled the roads of Spain.

It was the next day that, quite out of the blue, I think I made history and possibly qualified for an entry into the Guinness *Book of Records*.

Travelling back with my bike from Oliva, a town close to where I have my apartment, I passed the entire Radio Shack squad of 18 riders, Lance Armstrong et al, who were time-trialling in groups of six, accompanied by two escort cars.

They were moving at around 25 mph, but I cruised past them with ease, probably the first man within six months of drawing his old-age pension and six days after laser surgery who had ever overtaken the greatest cycling legend in the history of sport – and with a bike too big and gears on the frame. Chapeau, eh?

Now I am not one to boast or dwell on minute detail, so I will conclude the historic moment by admitting that I was actually driving a Fiat Panda at the time; and my cycle was resting on the back seat.

I know that, to a degree, that is irrelevant, so all that needs to be remembered is that your author annihilated a seven-times winner of the Tour de France when out with his bike. Eat your heart out Bradley Wiggins.

The next day, I was back at hospital for my final examination and the news that I had been waiting for: my eye problem had improved sufficiently for me to be able to fly home to England, albeit 10 days later than planned.

Within 24 hours I was back on home soil after two weeks of enforced boredom and just 45 minutes of cycling under my belt.

Oh, and the scalp of Lance Armstrong.

The First 50 Miles

ONE week after my ill-fated excursion to Spain I set myself my biggest challenge to date – my first 50-mile solo ride.

Yes, I am sure that this revelation will be met with sneers and skyward glances from many of you , as there are countless thousands of weekend enthusiasts undertaking this minor feat every Sunday, many before breakfast with their cycling caps set at a jaunty angle and a fag behind one ear.

But for me it was, if you will excuse the pun, a personal mountain I had to climb. With three months to go before my LEJOG departure I had to know my current state of fitness.

While I was aware it would mean pain, I was also aware it would be absolute pleasure as the anticipated 50 miles threaded me through some of the most picturesque villages in the Cotswold Hills.

So, on a cold but beautifully sunny February Saturday it was with a little trepidation and much anticipation that I set off from my Chadlington home and ventured through Wychwood Forest down into Swinbrook and on through to the picture-postcard town of Burford. Continuing south along deserted single-track lanes the rolling countryside levelled out, and I was able to breeze through Westwell, Holwell and Eastleach without the usual reminder from my thighs that my personal lactic acid plant was just about to go into full production.

Between Hatherop and Coln St Aldwyns I hastened upon a traditional rustic scene that probably hadn't changed in well over 100 years. The first clue came when I passed three shire horses grazing on the grass verge.

Then turning a corner, in front of me was the little piece of our English heritage that I had almost forgotten – two brightly painted traditional Romany caravans set in a small copse of trees close to a babbling stream; rarefied beauty, so simple and yet so moving.

It was a sight that compared in solitude and tranquillity with John Constable's 'Hay Wain' or maybe one of William Turner's landscapes and perfectly captured the Englishman's right to roam in the land of the free. My eyes scanned the scene for a glimpse of a weather-beaten, gnarled wood carver whittling another fine wooden masterpiece to sell at the next Craft Fair on his travels; or maybe a sighting of his wife, in long flowing skirt, billowing blouse, jet black tresses fringed with enormous brass earrings, perched over a cauldron of bubbling rabbit stew.

Alas, it was not to be, I had got too far ahead of myself. It was not the traditional free spirited couplet following age-old customs that I had imagined, more apprentices, pursuing a mobile lifestyle away from the urban pressures of life. No whittling wood, no earrings, not even a well-thumbed Ray Mears book on 'Survival in the Wild'. Alas, the reality and the dream were light years apart.

My romantic notions were further dashed when I spotted close by a 1950s khaki-coloured army surplus tent with the flaps open, displaying a rather unkempt woman with lower clothing akimbo sitting astride a large white pot. It was abundantly clear that she was not expecting guests. I wobbled slightly as I gazed at this highly intimate interface between two apprentice travellers and nature, before dropping down a couple of gears and accelerating away to safety. There was no way I was going to be accused of the worst kind of rural voyeurism.

As I dropped into Bibury 10 minutes later, I was still turning the images over in my mind, eventually concluding that my overactive interest in country culture had placed me in an uncompromising situation that I was lucky to escape from. I conceded that I had been unfortunate, too inquisitive and certainly wrong to stare – but in fairness I was not solely responsible. If the woman had kept her flaps firmly shut on her gear, none of this would have happened.

It would be a pleasure to record that the sights and sounds of the remainder of my mini marathon ride through the chocolate-box hamlets of Sherbourne, Windrush, Great Barrington and Taynton erased the memory of canvas latrines, but if I did I would be lying. Even a hardened Boy Scout would have blushed.

However, setting aside a person of the fairer sex completing her ablutions, it was a minor thrill to arrive back home some four hours later with my first 55-mile ride completed. It was an early milestone to record and the first major sign that I was capable of travelling more than 25 or 30 miles in a day.

What was now needed were a couple of 'back-to-backs' with a total mileage exceeding 100 to check whether I had the stamina to match the enthusiasm.

The good news was that I was making progress.

LANDS END - JOHN O'GROATS

BETTY HILL
JOHN O'GROATS
CRASK INN
EVANTON
GRANTOWN-ON-SPEY
GLENSHEE
KELTY
TUSHIELAW INN
LAZONBY
BASHALL EEVES
MIDDLEWICH
BROCKTON
HILLERSLAND
CHEDDAR
SOUTH MOLTON
WADEBRIDGE
LANDS END

Goodbye Chadlington

EARLY mornings in the Cotswolds, at the start of a new summer's day are invariably beautiful, the panoramic view from my bedroom window across the Evenlode Valley rarely failing to delight me. And Thursday, May 27 2010 was no exception. But this particular day was different, a lot different.

It was different because it was the day that I had been building towards for over six months, the day when the talking stopped. I was leaving the comfort of my home in the Oxfordshire village of Chadlington to ride solo from Land's End to John O'Groats. Six months of training, both indoors and on the road had been completed, cycling clothing purchased, accommodation booked, route agreed, and, nearing the age of 65, I was about to find out if I was full of bluster and bullshit or whether I had it in me to ride alone from the south-west corner of England to the north-east extremity of the Scottish mainland.

In the days leading up to my departure the major issues had revolved around what gear to take and what to leave behind. I was adamant that I did not want to exceed a weight of 24 lb in my panniers, this petty desire eventually being achieved after innumerable trials packing and unpacking equipment. The bathroom scales must have been seriously pissed off with their extra workload with, first me, then me and two panniers jumping on and off them as if it were a trampoline.

Following breakfast and a last-minute check, then recheck of equipment, you know all the lines, the best one being not to forget my bike, I drove with my wife, Christine, the 35 miles to Cheltenham to catch the train to Penzance. For an old codger a few months off retirement age

I felt remarkably calm and in control, the warm sunny day, picture-postcard scenery of Burford and spectacular countryside taking my mind off what lay ahead. Even the A40 was tolerable.

After exchanging hasty goodbyes with Christine (I was never one for passionate clinches in public, or private come to that), I walked tentatively down the steps on to the platform of Cheltenham's Lansdown station for the first time in 47 years.

As a skinny youth I travelled every winter Saturday for three years to Derby, to play in one of their junior sides before turning professional and enjoying another four years until a certain Brian Clough arrived and, after evaluating my miserable skills, suggested that I may like to find gainful employment elsewhere. Not quite the phrase he used, he favoured a more succinct one, one that left me in no doubt that his decision was non-negotiable.

Stepping on to the platform was like stepping back in time, almost half a century of time. The same iron posts supporting the same dirty glass roof, the same archaic bridge between the platforms that begged the Dulux paint company to satisfy its thirst. The same creaking, hanging sign welcoming newcomers to Cheltenham Spa, even a suspicion of the same Capstan Full Strength dog-ends resting neatly in the cracks of the concrete beneath my feet. Was that a hacking chesty cough I heard or just the faint breeze whistling through the parcels exit door? Who knows? My money would be on a porter puffing on a crafty Woodbine.

Yes, there were minor embellishments; a precariously placed glass waiting room, a digital monitor visually advising passengers of the inevitable 12-minute delay due to a herd of cows crapping on the line north of Worcester and a new chocolate vending machine, no doubt dispensing the same Tiffin bars that withstood all weathers in those halcyon days of the early 1960s.

Regardless, it was my home town station and amazingly ironic that after living in Derby, London, Cambridgeshire, Warwickshire and now Oxfordshire, I would be starting my geriatric adventure from the same place as where I began my adult life back in 1964. Do you know, I felt a little nostalgic, the tired station bringing back so many memories.

The train arrived, together with 3 million squashed flies hitching a free lift south on the engine's nose and windscreen, and after boarding I was able to give a very passable impression of Rod Hull wrestling with Emu when endeavouring to strap my bike to the metal frame provided adjacent to the washroom. Within 10 minutes this mini battle was over, and, clutching my two panniers and with a copy of the *Daily Mail* wedged firmly under my chin, I waddled down a full to overflowing carriage dressed in my freshly laundered Lycra.

Now, I am not saying I didn't look a complete and utter prat, but let me just leave you with the thought that I occasionally help them when they are short-staffed. However, it was unfortunate that I did not quite catch the comments of a couple of acned teenagers as I searched for my seat, neither did I join in the laughter that followed, especially when it dawned on me that I had suddenly become the centre of attention for the entire carriage. I could not be certain that the joke was at my expense, so I was prepared to give the last of Lord Snooty's Bash Street gang the benefit of the doubt.

However, if the crack had been about me, in my mind's eye I would have knocked 10 bags of shit out of them both before finishing with: 'By the way losers, Lance Armstrong sends his regards'. Either that, or after blushing profusely, hastily sit down and hide behind my newspaper. OK, it would have been option two. I can honestly say that as we sped through Longlevens, I got no satisfaction from seeing them lose a verbal joust with the ticket collector over travelling on children's tickets.

The journey, south-west through Gloucester, Bristol, Taunton and Exeter was the perfect way to prepare for my ride. I alternated between reading my newspaper and recalling happy times when I visited towns that were flashing by in my previous life as Operations Director of Lunn Poly Holiday shops. Then, when I became bored with both, just gazing out at the English countryside trying to imagine what life had in store for me over the next couple of weeks.

Soon after Exeter, the train hit the south Devon coast and made its way along probably the most picturesque line to be found anywhere in Britain. It followed the west bank the of the River Exe, then ran alongside the English Channel through Dawlish and Teignmouth before turning inland to Newton Abbott.

By now the sun was high in the sky and long white wispy clouds – which until now I had thought could be found only in New Zealand – were aimlessly drifting by. I can only conclude that the clouds were either completely lost or on holiday.

Couples were strolling along the sea wall, many of them looking for a cosy corner to enjoy some privacy , judging by the position of their hands. Men of all ages were scavenging, knee deep in the grey riverbank mud, hands searching for other treasures that males like between their fingers. It was all so quintessentially English. In fact it was such a delightful panorama, so relaxing and peaceful, that I almost forgot the tuna sandwiches that Christine had diligently packed for me along with two Jaffa cakes and a Mars bar. God that woman loves me.

My world was perfect as the train pressed on through Torquay, except for my memory recalling the last time I visited the English Riviera, for the funeral of a good business friend, Hiley Edwards, who had sadly departed from us a year earlier. Besides having a great sense of humour, never failing to laugh at my jokes, Hiley had the distinction of playing nearly 100 times for Devon in Minor Counties cricket, skippering the side at Lord's in 1991 in the knockout final against Staffordshire.

After changing trains in Plymouth I travelled on to Truro, where I had my first 'experience'. Now let me say right away, I am as broad-minded as the next person, I have to be when defending my wife's right to be a teacher of line dancing. Not an easy battle to win with some of my quick witted mates who seem to think that anyone interested in that type of musical physical activity has to have the body of Dolly Parton. I've even worked in Birmingham for a short time and driven through Handsworth alone at night, so I'm no pussycat.

Nevertheless, even I was taken aback by the aberration that alighted and eased himself into an aisle seat diagonally opposite mine. To make matters worse, we were the only occupants of the carriage. Me, a pensioner wearing Lycra and a 30-something male with shoulder length hair combed over a bald pate, attired in pink sunglasses, day-glo orange canvas jacket and blue shorts. An Errol Flynn moustache and two gold earrings topped off his appearance. To cap all that, I had also noticed that, on entering the carriage, he had entwined his bike round mine in a very sensual way. He settled, flashed a toothy smile, chirruped a rather cavalier 'Hi' and gave me the definite impression that he was on the lookout for a perverted sporting foursome - him, two bikes and me.

Although I was born and bred a raging heterosexual and married for over 40 years, I risked a fleeting friendship by returning his smile and rather coyly dropped my eyes to the floor. In my confused state my gaze wandered, eventually coming to rest at my new friend's feet. Oh no, please no. Not only was he wearing 'Jesus sandals', each of his toenails was sporting emerald green nail varnish. Trust me, his appearance would have given a village idiot a run for his money at a fancy dress party.

Truro to Redruth can only be 11 miles, maybe 15 minutes by rail, but they were the longest 15 minutes of my life. It was sheer bliss when he jumped up, smirked mischievously then bade me farewell with a less than manly 'Byee', before disentangling his bike from mine and mincing off down the platform. My first question to myself was, what was he doing out? It was still light and kids were due out of school. I mean, really!

But what upset me most was not the way he was dressed, not his effeminacy, not even the way he laid his Raleigh on my virgin bike. It was the fact that he had no nail varnish on his fingers to complement his toes. In my world there is no excuse for slapdash presentation. Will I telephone him? Probably not – but I will write.

At 4.30 p.m., and on time, the train arrived in Penzance and I headed out on the A30 for the 9-mile ride to Sennen and my first bed and breakfast accommodation at the Sunnybank Hotel, high on the cliffs overlooking Sennen Cove.

Hosts Eleni and Bernard Durrant made me very welcome and in

conversation suggested I eat at the Beach restaurant, right on the sands about a 10 minute stroll away. We continued with small talk, Bernard a staunch Cornish Pirates rugby fan, telling me of his desire to emigrate to New Zealand. However, he also told me that he was having a problem persuading Eleni to do so, even though their two children were keen. Having visited the country on two occasions and finding it incredibly beautiful, I was in the Bernard camp and proceeded to give Eleni a tourist board promotional presentation, only stopping just short of performing the Maori Haka as a conclusion to my performance. Feeling rather pleased that I had been able to offer my assistance and advice, I then set off for some food, even though I did feel a slight tinge of guilt when I heard raised voices coming from the house as I walked down the path. Quite logically, following my input, I passed it off with the thought that they were arguing whether to settle in North or South Island. I also consoled myself with the thought that my expert travel advice had helped a young family plan where they would spend the rest of their lives together. Once a travel man always a travel man.

Sennen Cove has everything you could want from a Cornish cove. A long sandy beach, smart restaurant, a pub that sells Cornish pasty, peas and chips for under £6.00 and a free floor show from surfers who leave offices early to catch the evening waves. After downing a cold Skinner's Cornish lager I chose the Beach restaurant. If it was good enough to regularly look after the culinary needs of Alan Titchmarsh, Tess Daly and Vernon Kay it was good enough for me. Or, like me now, was my waitress shamelessly name-dropping?

The downside of residing in a hotel overlooking a cove is the walk back, especially after consuming paté, loin of pork, sticky toffee pudding and two more Skinner's. I chose the cliff path and, on more than one occasion, nearly aborted my 'End-to-End' ride before even seeing Land's End due to me stupidly following a route which a mountain goat would turn up his nose at. Good fortune and crawling on all fours saved me the embarrassment of dropping in on late diners below, and, after 20 sweat-soaked minutes, it was good to see the lights of my overnight hostelry.

I decided it was prudent to retire to my room immediately, thus avoiding any further travel questions being thrown at me. It was also very quiet. By 10 o'clock I was in bed asleep, dreaming about the route I would take to Wadebridge the next day.

For some reason I slept badly, tossing and turning fretfully. Continually in my mind came the same two questions. Firstly, should I take the A30 from Land's End or stick to B roads and lanes? And, secondly, would I have a problem navigating my way through Christchurch, Wellington and Auckland? As Christine would have said: 'Why did you have to get involved ... ?'

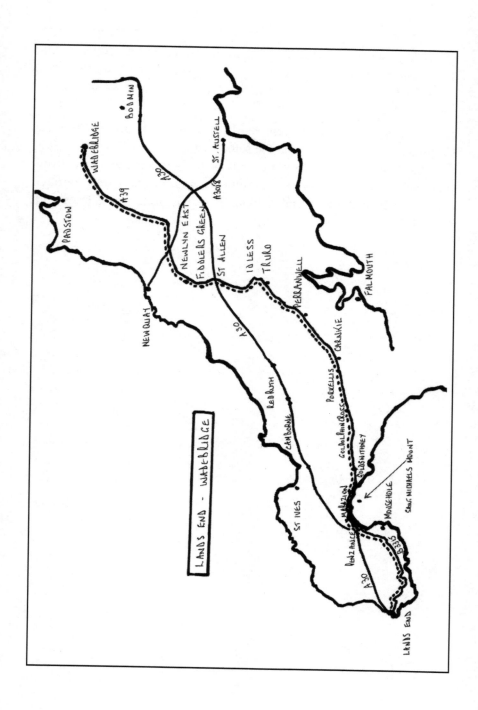

LANDS END - WADEBRIDGE

Day 1
Land's End to Wadebridge

AFTER a very quiet breakfast and even quieter kitchen I left Bernard and Eleni to their domestic and international differences with the immortal words, 'Thank you very much, I will let you know if I get there'. Whether they interpreted 'there' as John O'Groats or Dunedin I could not be sure, but I had other things on my mind, the beginning of the first day proper of my epic ride.

In no time at all I arrived at Land's End and rode confidently through the arch of the small shopping centre in search of the famous signpost that provided mileages to New York, the Isles of Scilly and John O'Groats. Rather cleverly, I thought, I chose the latter direction. And I did for two reasons. The first because I had booked bed and breakfasts all through Great Britain and did not like wasting money and secondly, the road conditions to the former two did not look great. A tad flooded I thought.

It was 8.30 a.m. and another beautifully warm sunny day with little breeze, perfect for my 71-mile first leg to Wadebridge. Standing alone next to the sign I looked out across the Atlantic remembering some of the celebrities who had stood on this very spot before or after just completing LEJOG.

Dr Barbara Moore was my first recollection, walking the distance in the 1960's and more recently, in 1985, Sir Ian Botham completing his 900-mile walk in aid of leukaemia research.

A man named Butler is the current holder of the cycling record, in

2001 riding 870 miles in a rather sluggish 1 day 20 hours 4 minutes and 20 seconds – about the time it would take me to get out of Cornwall. I consoled myself by knowing that Mr Butler had a support car to carry his panniers, as did Jango Cann who was only seven years and nine months when he rode 'End-to-End' in 2002.

Even Andy Rivett's running record was safe from my grasp, with him completing the course in a brisk nine days and two hours. Top honours though must surely go to nine year old Joe Lambert, a diabetic, who walked the distance in 40 days, averaging over 22 miles a day, while at the same time raising £5,000 for diabetes research.

After reflecting that I would not be erasing anyone's name from the *Guinness Book of Records* I turned to study the West Country Shopping Village more closely. That is, if three shops selling local produce, clothing and tatty souvenirs constitute a village.

I racked my brains to try and visualise something even more naff than this overtly graceless commercial venture perched on top of the cliff looking out to America, but failed miserably. As did the shopping village's architect.

Soon I was surrounded by around 20 cyclists, all in groups, some accompanied with a dad in his escort car. There were two lads from Morecambe and Darwin trying to beat 10 days and for a few minutes they were my new best friends, swapping training stories as well as the best route north.

Suddenly they were gone, replaced by Richard Catlin and his partner. Richard is an old a friend from my home village who had settled in Newlyn on the outskirts of Penzance. It was kind of both of them to drive down to see me off and even kinder to take a few photographs of me making my departure.

With a cheery wave to Richard, at precisely 9.04 a.m. I set off on my long journey, glad to be free from the fast growing number of cyclists and, yes, excited to be on my way.

The suns rays were already warm and within half a mile of my departure point I stopped briefly to shed my outer riding jacket. Seconds after remounting I was overtaken by three riders travelling at twice my speed, presumably intent on having a late breakfast in Bristol, lunch in

Manchester and catch the six o'clock news somewhere north of Edinburgh. They probably wouldn't be in John O'Groats until mid afternoon tomorrow at the earliest.

My temporary lapse of confidence caused by the boy racers was restored when I remembered reading about some LEJOG folklore involving a snail and a tortoise competing against each other in a race that started at Land's End in April 1954. Tortoise was last sighted in April 2010 approaching Penzance, but sadly the snail's effort ended in tears, being crushed by a baby's buggy seconds after being photographed next to the signpost at Land's End. Ironically, he now holds the record for the shortest ever attempt at an 'End-to-End' – a feat that is unlikely to be smashed – quite literally.

The route from Land's End recommended by the Cycling Touring Club took me almost immediately on to the B3315 for the slightly lengthier 12-mile ride into Penzance.

Within four miles I was introduced to my first Cornish 'slope' and my bike introduced to its lowest gear. It was like trying to ride up a circular helter-skelter. The road bent sharply to the left, and there was no way I was going to stay tight to the left and keep moving forward, I would have grazed my nose on the road. Instead, I veered to the wrong side of the road before veering left and rode across the slope. Dangerous you may say – but very effective.

Fortunately the rest of the leg to Penzance was sheer joy, travelling at a steady 14 mph through open fields and woodland interspersed with high banked grassy hedgerows overflowing with buttercups, bluebells, red campions, foxgloves and sporadic bushes of yellow gorse. It really was a perfect introduction to my first day on the road – pure heaven.

A former business colleague, Colin Wilson, who I was to meet later on the ride, told me I simply had to visit the resort of Mousehole, the home of the Penlee Lifeboat whose entire crew of eight perished in hurricane-force winds on a fateful day in December 1981. Colin's a great character and lives in a 'blue sky' world, every resort he travels to being fantastic, the best place on the planet. Naively, I used to believe him, well that is until he came back from Malta and told me that it was his *'numero uno'* resort of all time. Now I stick to trawling the internet for my ideas.

Anyway, it was a suggestion that I sadly had to reject especially after my experience scaling Mount Everest's cousin a mile or two back. I took the view that the hill out of 'Muzzle' would be of a similar gradient only much longer and I had a further 60 miles to ride. If the many hills ahead of me were to be as steep as the one just scaled I would not have time for sightseeing.

After an hour I dropped down a steep descent into Newlyn and on into Penzance. Close to the sea wall I acknowledged two senior citizen cyclists, who looked as though they were practising for a slow bicycle race. With a slightly overconfident and breezy 'Good morning' I flew past them before heading east along the dual carriageway to Marazion.

The view out across Mounts Bay was stunning, made all the more attractive by the sight of St Michael's Mount standing tall and proud half a mile off-shore. At high tide it is cut off completely from the mainland, its only surface access by causeway at low tide. It has a resident population of just 34, some of them children who travel every day to Marazion to attend school. Not many kids can be told by their parents as they are waved off to class: 'Don't walk home on your own, unless the tide's out'.

I pulled into a coach park to get a better view of St Michael's Mount and take photographs. A couple were already there and their faces were vaguely familiar. Yes, the same couple that I had overtaken two miles back. While I had been dicing with death along the dual carriageway they had sauntered along the sea wall overlooking the beach. I smiled as they looked my way but somehow felt that their cheery 'Good morning again' was slightly over the top and a touch arrogant.

I pressed on up the hilly main street of Marazion, with its art and pottery shops in abundance, before disappearing once more into the country lanes that wind through Goldsithney, Millpool, Goldolphin Cross and Releath, stopping for an early lunch after climbing up the short hill into Porkellis.

I was 28 miles from Land's End; it was 11.45 a.m., hot, and the Star Inn beckoned. My, was that lager shandy thirst-quenching. For strictly medicinal purposes it crossed my mind to add another and some lunch too.

Why not? I only had just over 40 miles to travel and it was not yet midday.

I summoned the menu and perused it carefully under the watchful stare of the young barman. Eventually, after deciding on the pasta course I waved him over so he could take my order. His first words were somewhat surprising. There was no food available on this particular lunchtime, as the chef had gone fishing.

Now, there are a couple of issues here. Who employs a barman who hands you a menu, lets you select a dish and then tells you nothing is available? And secondly, who employs a chef who is sitting comfortably in his boat in the bay while his customers go hungry. I don't care if his catch is fresh for his evening diners – I'm allergic to fish.

I asked the barman if he would mind if I ate the Jaffa bars and Kendal Mint Cake I had brought with me. He spread his two palms skywards, shrugged his shoulders and pouted his lips, a stance that I interpreted as a classic Cornish 'Am I bothered?'

The outer wrapping of the Jaffa bar was soon removed.

I left my understaffed oasis and continued in perfect solitude through Carnkie and Stithins literally and metaphorically full of the joys of spring. The weather was perfect, the flowers in full bloom, the bike and its occupant fit and well. And to cap it all, I was ahead of schedule for my journey to Wadebridge. Life was good.

Well, it was until I hit Perranwell and saw the longest, steepest hill in the whole of the Northern Hemisphere. I swear it made Porlock Hill look like the Fens. It was so steep the potholes could be converted into caves for homeless troglodytes.

It has to be recorded that my pace was rather pedestrian, no, correction, rather less than pedestrian; I could have crawled up the incline quicker. But I refused to crawl, or walk, and by standing and sitting, by huffing and puffing, and by convincing myself that the summit was just round the next corner I made it. With a satisfied smile and bursting lungs I headed on for Truro.

As I rode I reflected on the Perranwell hill and estimated that if I travelled up every hill at 5 miles per hour and down every one at 30 miles an hour, starting and ending at sea level , I would be in pain from climbing for 85 per cent of the time and in fear of death from the other 15 per cent. As I entered Truro on a busy Friday lunchtime I concluded that life wasn't fair on occasions.

It also flashed through my mind that the man with the emerald green toes may be back and lying in wait for me, possibly a deep-rooted distraction which caused me to misread my directions and end up on the cobbled pedestrian streets of the city at precisely the same time as at least four million shop and office workers were seeking their lunchtime pasty.

Cycling slowly in cleats, the contraption that locks your feet to the pedals, is not to be recommended at any time and certainly not when half of Cornwall requires lunchtime sustenance. Some of the words directed at me as I wobbled through them I hadn't heard since my old Scout Master tripped over a guy rope when leaving Akela's tent only a few hours after we had arrived at camp. I can clearly recall that we had made a promise to do our duty to God and the Queen and be kind to animals. I often wondered whether my old SM did his duty that night.

Truro is the administrative capital of Cornwall with a population of 20,000, with notable former residents being Matthew Etherington, the Stoke City footballer, and Roger Meddows-Taylor, the drummer with Queen. Way before them was Barbara Joyce West, the second to last survivor from the RMS *Titanic*.

Here is my question. What do Truro and the Titanic have in common?

I'll tell you, lots of hysterical people running round in ever decreasing circles.

More by luck than judgement and with a continued wary eye on every cyclist, I managed to work my way to the north of the city and on to the lane for Idless. From there I encountered a seemingly endless roller coaster ride of country lanes through St Allen, Fiddlers Green, St Newlyn East and Whitecross, all of them confirming without doubt that my mathematical assumptions arrived at earlier had been spot on. It was definitely an 85:15 percentage ratio.

As I rode I recalled the very first time I had visited Cornwall, a family holiday to Chapel Porth near St Agnes, when I was four, maybe five. I remembered it well for a very good reason. Our holiday home was a wooden chalet situated on a sandy path close to the beach, and in the chalet next door lived a woman with a billowing blouse and skirt. She also had a parrot as a pet.

The immortal words: 'Don't put your finger in the cage' will stay with me forever; they've already clocked up 60 years. Alas, health and safety guidelines were but a dream and parental control lax in those days. As soon as everybody's back was turned in my finger went. It came out bloody quicker than it went in albeit minus most of the flesh from my third finger of my right hand.

I still boast a rather attractive half-inch scar to this day as a result of childhood disobedience. However, not quite so visible as the one I would incur very soon.

After over two hours and 20 miles of hard climbs and descents I crossed the fast flowing busy A39, a major road that begins in Falmouth before following the northern coastlines of Cornwall and Devon all the way up to Barnstaple. More importantly, I saw that it bypassed Wadebridge, my first night stop.

So what was it to be for me, the pretty flower festooned quiet hilly lanes that wandered through some of the most attractive countryside in Britain or the faster, flatter, busy white-knuckle ride on one of the counties major arteries? Hills or noise? For anyone with a brain it was no contest really. The A39 it was.

It is surprising how quickly a cyclist can adapt to nose-to-tail traffic travelling at 80 mph and for 50 minutes I risked life and limb as I closed in on my first night's resting house. In honesty the A39 was not too bad as it contained a cycle lane about two yards wide. Theoretically it worked well but not when idle motorists throw an array of empty coke bottles, MacDonald's Big Mac boxes, lager cans (Carlsberg appearing to be the holidaymakers favourite) and other unwanted food and beverage wrappings on to the roadside. For novice cyclists it becomes a death defying slalom ride much to the entertainment of passing vehicles. And that's before you take into consideration other detritus such as stones, gravel and used tyres. By way of contrast, however, it was direct and as the saying goes, mustn't grumble.

After suggesting to too many passing motorists who came close that they may wish to commit an impossibly difficult sexual act upon themselves I left the A39 to them and was soon cycling downhill into, what was on May 28 2010 at 3.50 p.m., my favourite town in the world – Wadebridge. That accolade was endorsed when I stopped to ask the first pedestrian I saw if they knew where Spring Gardens in Bradford Quay was situated. 'Everyone knows where the mayor lives,' I was told. Within two minutes I was there and knocking on the mayor's door. How many Town Mayors do you know who run a Bed and Breakfast? Probably the same number as me now.

My double room was perfect and so was the bath I lounged in as I reflected on the fact that I had just completed my longest ever ride, a distance of 71 miles in a shade over six hours. Not half bad considering the terrain. Fortunately, while my odometer recorded a fastest speed of 40 mph, it was not sophisticated enough to record my lowest speed coming uphill out of Perranwell.

Spring Gardens, my B&B, was an old merchant's house dating back to 1670, with Jenny Knightly, my landlady and her husband, Steve (both keen cyclists), doing bed and breakfast for the past 15 years. And very well they do it too.

Jenny was also very good at directions, suggesting that I may like to dine at The Ship, a pub less than 100 yards from her doorstep where, I was told, I could eat well and eat cheaply. So just after 5 p.m., a freshly laundered sexagenarian sporting a superior smile and refreshed limbs strolled the short distance for his first well-earned pint of real ale of his adventure.

The pub was busy, with many of the customers having an end of week drink on their way home from work. Many others had clearly left work at lunchtime and were still thirsty. It suited me to fade into the background, watch cricket on TV, while at the same time listen to the absolute rubbish people talked when full to overflowing with ale.

The walls of the pub held posters promoting a Nigel Cassidy charity and I was intrigued to know if it was the same person who had played football for Norwich City, Scunthorpe, Oxford United and Denver Dynamos. The barmaid confirmed that it was and although Nigel had died, the pub was run by his son and Nigel's wife, Shelley.

I thought no more of it until about 20 minutes later when Shelley introduced herself to me and told me a little about Nigel's life. I told her that a friend of mine, Ken Skeen, a boyhood chum from Cheltenham, had played for Oxford around Nigel's time and was amazed to learn that not only did she know Ken and his wife, Diane, but that they had been down to the pub many times.

We chatted away merrily until Shelley had to leave, but not before she opened her purse and gave me £20.00 for the charity I was riding for. Can you believe just how kind a gesture that was, a generous donation given to a total stranger to support a charity she had never heard of until a few moments earlier? Next time you are in Wadebridge, look her up – she's a lovely lady.

It was soon after that two more end-to-end cyclists came in, coincidentally also staying at Spring Gardens. One of them,Guy, sold ballet floors worldwide and had once had the misfortune to be imprisoned briefly in Kazakhstan for trying to pass his Oyster card off as ID instead of his passport, while Jason's claim to fame was when he rode in the 2009 Naked Ride in London. As fate would have it, I would hear more about Jason later on my ride.

Good food, good beer and pleasant company. What more could I desire? I left the pub with the distinct feeling that I could get used to this way of life. It even crossed my mind to relay that fact to my wife via one of those humorous Donald McGill's saucy postcards.

Sleep came easy that night, but not before I played the day over again in my mind. 71 miles at close on 12 mph, over some of the toughest hills on the ride.

Seemed easy enough. What could possibly go wrong?

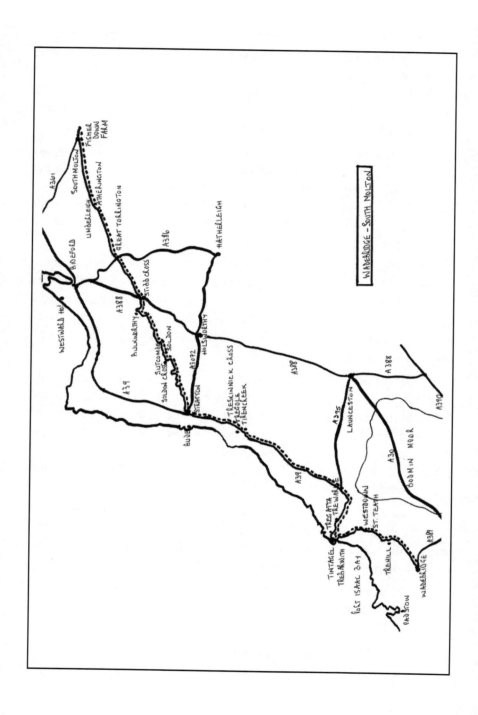

WADEBRIDGE – SOUTH MOLTON

Day 2
Wadebridge to South Molton

FIRST in the bathroom is always the first challenge of the day in most B&Bs and that was achieved comfortably due to Guy and Jason lingering perhaps a little longer than they should have the night before in the The Ship.

After an excellent breakfast and an exchange of pleasantries with the Lord Mayor, I left Wadebridge under an overcast sky for the long haul to South Molton, just south of the Exmoor National Park. I had enjoyed my short stay in the home town of Andrew Ridgeley, of Wham fame and where Jethro had lived for many years (he did, honestly, I'm not joking), and rode up the long hill past the football ground to rejoin the A39.

Fortunately it was a short stay on the trunk road as I was soon turning towards Trelill, a small village 3 miles from Port Isaac Bay. From there more country lanes took me on to St Teath and an introduction to the laid back ways of the Cornish transport authorities.

Travelling down a lane at something approaching 35 mph, I reached the bottom and was looking forward to a good few yards of roll uphill until I needed to pedal. Instead I ground to a standstill, which could not have been matched if I had been driving a Formula 1 car into a sand trap. I stopped stone dead.

The local road authorities had very kindly tarred and gritted the road the previous day but, due to the Bank Holiday beckoning, had kindly left it unrolled and unloved until the coming Tuesday. Steamroller man had not been for turning and had presumably said: 'Tough, not my problem, see you next week,' or whatever the Cornish equivalent is.

It may not have been his problem (only his job), but it was mine as I had a 1 in 9 ascent to overcome with my tyres half an inch deep in Cornish granite. Miraculously, I not only managed to pedal to the top I also avoided the puncture that every sharp edged piece of gravel threatened to inflict.

Take my tip: avoid lanes on Bank Holiday weekends or make a quick call to the Cornish transport authorities and check what kind of mood Steamroller Ron is in. I can assure you it will not be a wasted call.

Let me move on.

All I can say is, that 'it' happened somewhere between Westdowns and Trebarwith but I can't be any more precise than that. I don't want to be; it brings back too many memories, all of them bad.

So many times I have watched the Tour de France and seen cyclists come off at high speed and wondered if it hurt and for how long. I need wonder no more for I was soon to be introduced to my first serious fall from a fast moving bike.

Cornish lanes are invariably high-sided with steep grass verges topped by a hedge, giving the traveller a tunnel effect but without the roof, and I was enjoying the thrill of a downhill section, travelling at around 35 mph when I saw, about 30 yards ahead, the lane bend round to the left. Not being able to see how tight the bend was I touched my rear brake to slow myself down. Tyres, loose gravel and speed are not natural bedfellows and my bike fell away to my right and I went down, hard and fast.

For 20 yards, although it felt like 200, I slid along the lane, cleverly using my left thigh and elbow as a brake. Eventually I reached the bend and came to a halt half way up the verge, the smell of burning flesh fresh in my nostrils.

My immediate thought was for my bike but a quick check showed that except for a scraped handlebar, everything was intact, the pannier having taken a lot of the impact. I was not quite so lucky and a visual check to where it hurt most showed a 3in-graze on my elbow, one the size of a small plate on my thigh and a deeply gashed thumb which was disgorging blood at the rate of at least a pint a minute. I had also ripped the sleeve of my brand new high-vis rain-jacket, something even more distressing than my wounds.

In a strange way, I felt comfortable, relaxed and in control. I rationalised my accident by convincing myself that all cyclists fall off and incur superficial injuries and I was no different. It had just happened to me on Day 2, while I was still 1,000 miles from my eventual destination. I was even able to raise a smile as I stood in that lonely lane in deepest Cornwall with cycling shorts round ankles: 'my meat and two veg' fully exposed, applying Savlon to my thigh.

'Yes son, tell that to the judge in court,' would have been the likely response from a prowling Panda car driver to my plea of innocence, but fortunately 'Plod' was not on patrol in my vicinity.

Within 10 minutes I was on the move and smiling again when three cars came towards me in quick succession. Fate had decreed that they had not come earlier and added their contribution to my self-inflicted injuries, or seen my impression of *'Indecent Exposure'*. Maybe things weren't quite so bad after all.

I metaphorically and literally limped the 5 miles into Tintagel and came by a coffee shop that was open. I entered, feeling confident that they could assist me with my injuries. You know what I mean; warm water, a fleecy towel, and fully stocked medical chest, lots of TLC, that sort of thing.

I locked the bike and with my panniers, entered the empty shop. A young girl in her mid-teens seemed to be the only person serving but it was immediately apparent that her induction training had not covered how to handle sodden cyclists, oozing blood from several orifices and dripping it on her newly scrubbed floor tiles.

Looking back, the surreal scene was enhanced by my misted-up spectacles that prevented me from making any 'eye-to-eye' contact with her. She did what anyone else would have done – she ran.

Seconds later from the back of the shop came an Indian gentleman wearing a brightly coloured turban. 'Bloody Hell, that's a bit strong,' I thought. Surely the cavalry should have been summoned first. This was quickly turning into a West End farce not helped by, presumably the proprietor, jumping up and down while waving the palms of his hands at me chanting: 'Oh no, no, no, no, no. Oh my goodness, no, no, no, no, no.'

Something deep inside me, instinct probably, told me he wasn't pleased to see me or for that matter the increasingly deep puddles my soaked panniers were making on his immaculate floor.

Tossing him a googly I said 'Any chance of a coffee?'

Off he went again, in what I assume was some kind of Sikh war chant, before he was able to gain a semblance of composure and ushered me out of the shop with the advice that there were public conveniences next door and I could clean myself there.

Off I went, and, sure enough, there were very clean facilities that suited me admirably. Within minutes I had washed my wounds and looked for paper towels to dry myself. There were none, only a hole in the wall that emitted hot air when hands were placed inside. This I did and a jolly good job it did too, so good that I decided to stick my head in the hole to dry my hair. Why not? It was free and I did want to look my best for my host next door.

The warm air was a Godsend and for fully a minute I bent double with my head in the hole. It would and should have been longer, but I became aware of someone behind me, a courteous clearing of his throat alerting me to his presence. My head shot out and I gave him a passable impression of Ken Dodd on a bad hair day. I suppose that with fresh blood dripping from my thigh and thumb I appeared a little bit manic.

Now, I am not normally one to be stuck for words but in this instance I was. We stared at each other for possibly five seconds, perhaps longer, before I broke the silence with 'I fell off'. Hardly descriptive I grant you, but sufficient for my Tintagel toilet visitor to turn on his heels and scuttle away without gaining the relief he was seeking. I wouldn't have been surprised if his first call wasn't to the local asylum to check whether they were missing anybody.

Returning to the still empty coffee shop, I passed the Indian medical check, sat with my coffee and studied the map. I was well behind time and was sick of hills. Out of the corner of my eye I noticed the Indian gentleman sidling up to my table with a sideways gait. He was wary to say the least. Maybe he had forgotten to check my finger nails for dirt? Or was he the Good Samaritan?

He asked me where I was going, but on reflection may have said when was I going. I told him that my route took me up the coast road to Boscastle, Widemouth Bay and Bude then across the A39 to Stratton. He advised against that plan due to the numerous descents and ascents through the many coves. His recommendation was to head inland through Tregatta and Trewarmett but going nowhere near Trefew, Tregoodwell or Trewassa or else I would be lost. I would then pick up the A39 further south that would take me north to Stratton.

I didn't fancy another session on the A39 but neither did I want the drudgery of further climbs especially in my fragile state. Being a local he knows best, I thought. And do you know something, he did.

The A39 was quieter than the day before and I was able to make good time, racing past signposts displaying the village names of Trencreek, Tregole and Treskinnock Cross and on into Devon.

It struck me as I passed the numerous signposts how hard it must be for a heavy drinker with a stutter to live in these parts. Can you imagine the scene outside a pub at chucking out time?

'You're in no fit state to drive, mate. Where do you live? I'll run you home.'

'Hic, I live in Tre, Tre, Tre, I live in Tre, Tre, Tre.'

I think if I had that unfortunate affliction, I'd move to a one-syllable place.

At Stratton I felt back in control and ventured off the A39 and into more lanes for my 15-mile ride north-east to Stibb Cross.

Unfortunately however, for the first but not the last time I became hopelessly lost in the maze of identical lanes. Gone were the villages of Trewisemen, Trebelclef and Trebormint (only joking but I bet they were there somewhere) to be replaced by Solden, Solden Cross, Sutcombe and Sutcombe Hill.

When I didn't think it could get any worse, it did, and I got bombarded with Kimworthy, Alfardisworthy, Dinworthy, Bulkworthy and Bradworthy, not forgetting Ashmansworthy and, best of all, Woolfardisworthy. Fortunately I stayed north of Chilsworthy and Holsworthy but believe me, if I had known they were there I would have paid them a visit.

Who makes these names up? I bet the village that sits astride the Cornwall/Devon border is called Treworthy – guaranteed.

For two hours my map and the signposts violently disagreed on my precise position. It would have been simpler directing me along yak tracks in Outer Mongolia or a footpath in the Gobi desert. It was so surreal it was becoming laughing matter. Only I wasn't laughing.

My day had changed from disaster to monotony. A 10 minute ride, stop, check the signpost pointing four different ways. Then check the map that refused to divulge any of them. Another 10 minute ride, another signpost, another map check and so it went on – two solid bloody hours of it. It was like nightmare, only one from which it was impossible to wake up. And all the time my thigh, elbow and thumb were reminding me that just because the bleeding had stopped, it didn't mean the pain had subsided.

Eventually I chanced upon Stibb Cross and regained my freedom. It was not exactly an oasis but it felt like one. It had a shop and there were people, two ladies at least. It was a start. I asked them the way to South Molton, my overnight stay, but both had recently moved from the north of England and were clueless. One was vaguely aware of Great Torrington though, seven miles away and as that was en route to South Molton I accepted the advice she gave me.

Warning them not to wander in the lanes south if they wanted to see their children grow up, I set off along the B3227, a motorway compared to where I had been. I was back on track.

Great Torrington is a historic market town (aren't they all?), famous for Dartington Crystal and the place where Henry Williamson based his 1927 novel, *Tarka the Otter*. Interestingly, in 1646 it hosted one of the largest battles of the Civil War, presumably over differences of opinion on village place names.

Crossing the River Torridge, I turned left, away from the town and rode on past the deserted five-storey Ambrosia Creamed Rice factory. It was a mess, sporting broken windows, hanging guttering and police signs warning intruders not to enter. It looked to me as though it was a building to escape from, not break in to.

It was clear that the produce along with the staff were long gone, confirmation to me that my cry to mother that my pudding had big lumps in had proved prophetically true and subsequently endorsed by the majority of the UK population.

The deserted site did nothing to help my spirits and I was feeling very low, having ridden nearly 60 miles in incessant rain. I had also shed half my body skin, been rejected by a coffee shop owner from Mumbai and been confused and bewildered by Devon's answer to Hampton Court Maze.

Averting my gaze from the building that had definitely produced its final pudding, I glanced back at the road to see, what I thought was an imitation of the Berlin Wall. Through rain flecked glasses it looked as though the B3277 had become Britain's busiest cul-de-sac. But, looking again, I saw it wasn't a wall but still a leaded road, albeit perpendicular, rising like the final stage of the ascent of Everest.

Boy, it was steep, so steep that pedestrians were walking up it roped together using crampons and ice axes. Packhorse mules were carrying their shopping.

Flat out I managed to maintain a speed of 6 mph and after inhaling just short of seven trillion breaths, I reached the top, exhausted but proud that I had conquered another challenge that had been presented to me. In fact, I quietly congratulated myself and I'm sure you will excuse me when I say it was my Ambrosian Moment.

There was a car park at the top and, as luck would have it, a stationary burger van that also sold coffee. By now it was late afternoon and all I had eaten since breakfast was some Kendal Mint Cake and a Jaffa bar. I was ready for a snack. My elation didn't last long though, for in a cruel moment of synchronised movement, precisely the second that I rode in, Burger man drove out. I never even had chance to loosen my cleats. One moment he was there and the next, in a cloud of blue smoke, gone, proof positive that his van was in need of a good service and the driver in need of a good slap.

When my bitterness had subsided I made a mental note that if ever I worked in the burger industry in this neck of the woods, 4.30 prompt on a Bank Holiday Saturday was the latest time I would make a sale.

If I thought the hill out of Torrington was steep it would turn out to be a doddle compared to the one leading from Atherington into Umberleigh. I am not exaggerating when I say I saw a motorcyclist crying by the side of the rode. Poor man was an acrophobic and just couldn't face it.

I empathised with his dilemma. With well over 60 hard miles in my legs and a thigh that was giving a passable impression of a nice leg of lamb, I was not amused to read a sign that warned: 'Slow down, steep hill ahead'. Any fool could see that. What it didn't say was: 'At the bottom it's payback time – so get peddling'.

Try to picture the scene, and I am not kidding here. A 1:4 gradient, rising seemingly forever into a grey leaden sky and a knackered 64-year-old frail, skinless man who had been forced to explore every last inch of every lane ever built in north Cornwall and Devon. And this seemed like the last straw, a hill that motorists wouldn't even attempt to scale unless their car had a minimum of a 3.5 litre engine and a full service history. And I was being asked to ride up it.

Sod it, game over. I walked.

It would be wrong of me to say I needed the exercise but there was no choice. Even walking was next to impossible with cleats on my cycling shoes and a heavy pack, and it was an age before I reached the summit and continued the short distance to South Molton and my overnight stay.

Fisher Down Farm, my B&B accommodation, was situated two miles outside the town and it wasn't long before I had settled in and was lying in a hot bath, replaying in my mind the day's adventures. Another little tip now: when half your thigh is a gaping wound, ease yourself into the bath's hot water slowly; anything quicker will result in a head wound and ceiling damage. I know, I was that pioneer.

Seventy-eight miles at a pathetic speed of 10.2 mph didn't start to tell the story. What it did tell me was that I had been on the road, alone, for nigh on seven hours, many of them totally lost, the majority with flesh wounds and almost all in driving rain. But I had survived, had a tale to tell, and was ,without question, better for the experience. Allegedly.

Di and Stan Colman, the owners of Fisher Down, were so kind to me it was hard to believe that I was anything other than family. Not only did Di take all my dirty washing, even the bloodied bits, but placed them in a symmetrically perfect pile outside my door the next morning, sparkling clean.

After I returned from dinner in South Molton, they even welcomed me into their private rooms to enjoy a couple of bottles of rosé wine while watching the Eurovision Song Contest. Don't laugh - it was what was needed.

Add an excellent full English breakfast to that and some sound advice from Stan on the best way to Taunton, for £20.00 in total, I think I might just have had a good deal.

One day I hope to return to Fisher Down to say thanks again for their marvellous hospitality. After the traumas of the day, it was much needed and gratefully received.

The result of the Eurovision Song Contest? We came bottom – again.

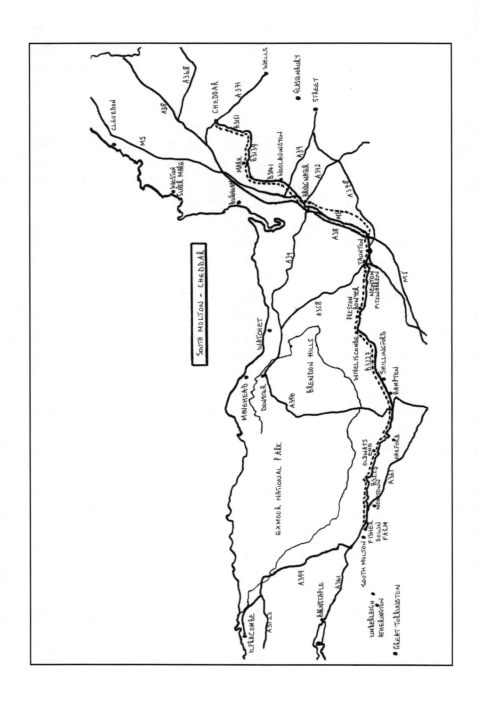

SOUTH MOLTON - CHEDDAR

Day 3
South Molton to Cheddar

BEFORE leaving Fishers Down Farm, Stan dissuaded me from following the Cycling Touring Club's recommended route across the lower slopes of the Exmoor National Park to Taunton, suggesting instead that the flatter A361 dual carriageway for a few miles before taking the B3227 cross-country through Bampton and Shillingford would better suit.

It wasn't that the CTC were wrong, it was more a case of having an easier day by excluding Exmoor following my tough ride up from Wadebridge the previous day.

I was very much looking forward to the day as I had arranged for my youngest son, Thomas, who was studying Civil Engineering at Kingston University, to join me in Bridgwater and ride the final 20 miles to my next overnight stop in Cheddar. He would then continue with me the next day when I was travelling over the Severn Bridge to follow the River Wye up into Monmouth. There my wife and a friend would meet us for dinner.

With the sun already warming the day, I left Di and Stan and was soon maintaining a consistent 15 mph on the A361, an excellent road that runs from the coast at Barnstaple before meeting with the M5 motorway just outside Tiverton. Being the fastest road to and from North Devon it is usually busy, but as it was early and a Sunday morning it was quiet with most of the South-West seemingly having a lie-in.

After a quarter of an hour, I turned on to the B3227 and started the long but steady climb through forestry land on my right while on my left enjoying the magnificent vista north towards the Exmoor Forest. Time was on my side as Thomas's train was not due to arrive in Bridgwater until after lunch.

Plans were quickly amended when he called to say that his train had been delayed so we agreed to meet at Taunton station, giving him an extra 15 miles or so riding and me more time to bore him with my heroic adventures from the previous day.

In many ways the ride from South Molton to Taunton was one of the best periods of the entire trip. I had come through a nightmarish previous day wet and wounded, but certainly wiser. But today, the weather was beautiful, the roads nicely undulating and I had all the time in the world to saunter up to Taunton to meet my son.

I felt really fit and, equally important, mentally relaxed as I absorbed everything that the Devon and Somerset countryside could offer. The pleasure of life had returned and I was back on song. Silly as it may seem, I even had time to shed a tear as I cruised along. Don't ask me why, I just did. Perhaps the emotions of the previous day just bubbled to the surface.

Fordingbridge came and went, as did Bampton, and I was soon at Shillingford where I took over the bus shelter as my very own pit stop and quenched my thirst and hunger with an energy drink and yet another bar of Kendal Mint Cake.

What could be better, the sun high in the sky, a mid-morning snack consumed and all the time in the world to take in the scene.

Two dog walkers strolled by and I had a desperately strong urge to tell them that in a week's time I would be in Edinburgh. Fortunately for them, I managed to restrain my 'attention-seeking boast', contenting myself with a boyish giggle and self-satisfying smirk as they passed by. I am more than confident that, to this day, there are two dog owners in Shillingford who refuse to take their pets on solo walks past the bus shelter on a Sunday morning – just in case they see a self-satisfied sniggering cyclist laughing to himself.

I could have sat there all day but, feeling slightly sick after gorging a whole bar of the Lake District's finest, I continued on my way to Taunton.

Ah, Kendal Mint Cake, a great energy boost but too heavy to carry more than a few bars the length of Britain. Rather cleverly, though, I had planned in great detail and, before leaving home, had sent small supplies of mint cake, Jaffa bars and energy drink powder together with route planners and maps to each of the B&Bs up the line. Clever or what?

Funny thing was that I couldn't keep up with my constantly increasing food chain and ended up giving most of it away. Even today I bet there are snotty-nosed kids in Bolton and Chorley, plus one or two just outside Blackburn, still gnawing on my surprise gifts: 'Aye, it right takes some shifting does that there Kendal snap.'

In no time at all I had ridden through Petton, Wivelscombe, Preston Bowyer, Hill Common and Norton Fitzwarren, the latter name so perfect for a solicitor handling gay marital disputes I thought.

Taunton was still asleep, the traffic easily navigable, and it wasn't long before I was outside the railway station, reflecting that even with my leisurely ride from South Molton I still had an hour to spare until Thomas arrived.

I wheeled my bike on to the platform, locked it to a bench that had seen better days – my guess, better days in the early 1970s – and dropped into the station cafeteria where for slightly less than I had paid for my previous night's B&B I purchased a fudge muffin and regular cup of coffee.

I felt sufficiently confident to consider asking the tired female refreshment attendant, who had also seen better days – circa 1927-31 is my estimate – what was the difference between a regular and, possibly, an irregular coffee but had second thoughts when I saw the state of her fingernails. Luckily for me tongs were still in fashion in this buffet bar, so my muffin was delivered hygienically. The moment passed without incident.

My mischievous thinking was telling me one thing, however. My confidence and spirit were well and truly back and I was ready for the rest of the ride. Yesterday's mishaps had been confined to history.

Thomas's train arrived bang on time, just 15 minutes late, and, after sharing the usual condolences about the age and punctuality of First Great Western trains, we were soon ready to leave.

An enquiry at the station ticket office for the best route to Bridgwater bore a marvellous reward. We were told that behind the station, across the car park, we would find the Bridgwater and Taunton Canal and it that would take us serenely, almost halfway to Cheddar. A real stroke of luck, as it would allow us to avoid the busy and potentially lethal A38.

The canal opened in 1827 linking the River Tone to the River Parrott, but fell into disrepair and was closed. Restoration was completed in 1994 and the canal still transports drinking water to the people of Bridgwater. Locks abound, as do swing bridges, marinas, houseboats, waterside pubs and restaurants and its water and banks are perfect places on a hot sunny Sunday afternoon for walkers, cyclists, fishermen, leisure crafts, and canoeists.

Now fully restored by British Waterways and Somerset County Council, the canal, its towpath and picnic areas are idyllic places, a total contrast to the A38 we had resigned ourselves to tackle.

I later found out that the canal towpath forms part of Route 3 of the national cycleway, a further endorsement that we had found a hidden gem completely by chance. From hell to heaven in just 24 hours I thought. Isn't life grand?

The canal towpath took us conveniently to the north-west of Bridgwater and after 15 minutes in brisk traffic on the A39 we turned north on to the B3141 then the B3139 for Cheddar.

From joining the canal in Taunton, right through to Bridgwater and then onwards on the B3151 through Marke, Wedmore, and Cheddar, the terrain was completely flat and an ideal opportunity for Thomas to find his cycling legs. It was 35 miles of easy riding for him and 71 miles for me. Close to being the perfect day.

We quickly found our overnight accommodation in Cheddar, but before retiring to our room to freshen up we accepted our landlady Ann's kind invitation of a cup of tea and a slice of home-made walnut and lemon cake.

We were directed to the parlour of her truly grand home and sat like naughty schoolboys waiting for Ann to return with her late afternoon refreshments.

Looking back, it was my fault that it was almost an hour before we were able to tuck into our cake and sip our tea. Rather foolishly I asked Ann a question about a series of earthen hills that seemed to spring up from nowhere on the flat plain we had ridden over on the final five miles into Cheddar.

Clearly Ann was very proud of her town and surrounding countryside. Or in desperate need of a natter. In hindsight I would say both, because what followed was a monologue that lasted fully 45 minutes.

During that time I was as fascinated by her body positions as I was her oration. She started by standing up as straight as a guardsman, before leaning against the arm of the sofa then dropping further to actually sit on the arm. Then, and rather cleverly if I may say so, she slid effortlessly on to the seat of the sofa and finally, seeing she had us exactly where she wanted us, finished her routine by slipping her legs underneath herself, ending up looking decidedly similar to the Little Mermaid that overlooks the water's edge in Copenhagen.

In diving parlance I would have rated it at the upper end of difficult manoeuvres; it was right up there with a triple somersault with pike. Deep down I suspected she had done it many times previous to our visit but it held me so enthralled I almost forgot to listen to what she was saying.

Her subjects ranged from the Drumlins, formed in the Ice Age, which satisfied my initial question, through to her being friendly with Frankie Howerd, who she first met when she was 18, I mused about the same time the Drumlins were formed then.

She briskly moved on to cover her grandfather's diary that contained a recipe on how to make the very best marmalade, closing with a wonderful story about guests smuggling puppies into their rooms. There may have been more but in the 45 minutes she had us under her spell I may have lost consciousness for a little while.

I was too frightened to glance over at Thomas fearing that he had lost the will to live and was certainly not brave enough to pour myself a cup of, by now, stone-cold tea or slide a slice of walnut and lemon down.

Eventually she began to slow and finished her performance by giving us a full and detailed briefing on every eating establishment in town, although she cheerfully admitted that she hadn't eaten in any of them.

Her encore, although to be fair to Thomas and myself we had not requested one, was to state that a gentleman friend of hers was coming over at 7.30 to show some sepia slides of historic Cheddar and we would be more than welcome to attend.

Sadly we had to decline, feigning that we had to go for a walk to remove the stiffness from our legs. Over a few beers we exchanged recollections of her lecture and, do you know, we had both remembered every subject to the very last detail.

Yet another lovely lady who it was my good fortune to meet and one who just loved company. She maintained a very impressive guest house too.

Strange thing was, not once did she mention the world-famous Cheddar Gorge less that half a mile from her B&B. Must have slipped her mind. Either that or she was saving it for our next visit.

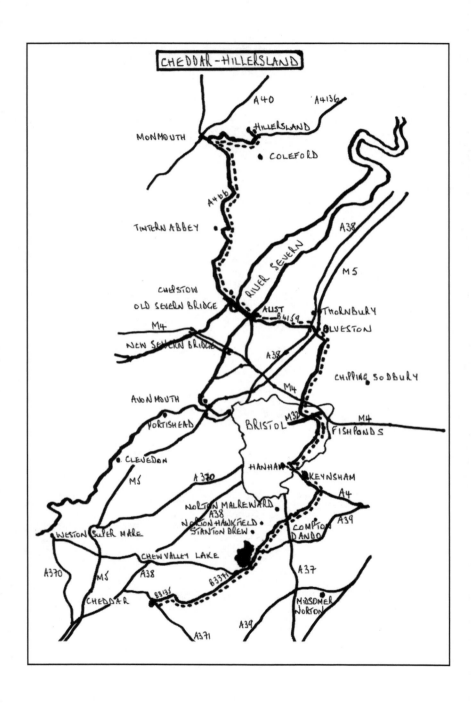

Day 4
Cheddar to Hillersland

THANKS to Ann's diligence, another full English breakfast had come and gone by just after eight o 'clock and we were on the road before nine for what would turn out to be the longest day of the ride. Over 80 miles, across deepest Somerset, round Bristol, into Wales and up into the Forest of Dean.

Within minutes we were at the mouth of one of the natural wonders of Great Britain – Cheddar Gorge. Consisting of limestone, the Gorge has a vertical face rising to a height of 450 ft. It is where Britain's oldest complete skeleton, named appropriately Cheddar Man, was found in 1903. Reputed to be 9,000 years old, it is rumoured that his last words were: 'Has Ann stopped rattling on about Frankie Howerd yet?' Climbing up through the Gorge was surprisingly easy, our pre-ride thoughts that it would be a killer being totally misplaced. As it happened it turned out to be a pleasant incline. The closest I came to dicing with death was when I toppled from my bike into stinging nettles when riding slowly for Thomas's photo call. Vanity works in mysterious ways.

We were soon out of the Gorge, with the B3371 taking us across the top of the Mendip Hills to West Harptree and magnificent views looking down and over Chew Valley Lake.

Thomas conveniently punctured so it gave me the opportunity to study the expanse of water that keeps the good residents of Bristol with such a vital commodity. It is the fifth largest lake in the UK and has been around for only 60 years. My research failed to reveal what the thirsty Bristolian citizens did for liquid before the lake was built – consume flagons of cider I suppose.

The lake is a haven for wild life and an internationally important site for wintering and migrating wild fowl. Figures show that 4,000 ducks (who counted those little sods?), 600 gold crested grebes and unknown numbers of sand martins, swallows, lapwings, common snipe, black headed gulls, red warblers and Eurasian coots all pass this way at some time during the year. That's a lot of birds and an awful lot of guano falling out of the sky.

Dropping several hundred feet (us not the bird excreta), we followed the east side of the lake before getting lost in the myriad of steep lanes around stately named villages such as Stanton Drew, Compton Dando, Norton Hawfield and, best of all, Norton Malreward. It was like reading the credits from the film *Gone with the Wind*.

On reflection it would have been far simpler to stay on the west side of Bristol as we were crossing the old Severn Bridge at Aust. The route that we were taking to the east and north was a nightmare of steep lanes and minimal directions, and we were soon hopelessly lost – again.

After much tutting and even more map studying, more by luck than judgement we eventually found ourselves on the A4 and rolling down the pleasant descent into Keynsham.

Keynsham is a place that will always remind me of my teenage years when the crackling airwaves of Radio Luxembourg regularly featured advertising by Horace Batchelor. Horace flogged his secret plans for winning a fortune on the old football pools; a magic formula, he would tell us, that couldn't lose. His ads always finished with: 'So write to me, Horace Batchelor at Keynsham, that's spelt K-E-Y-N-S-H-A-M and I will make you a millionaire.'

Now, my question is this: if Horace's plans were so bloody good, why didn't he keep his mouth shut, save on marketing costs, send all his formulas to the football pools companies himself and trouser the millions he was promising others? He would have become a billionaire. I don't know of any successes from people buying into Horace's master plan, but he certainly put Keynsham on the map. Nice one 'H.'

Keynsham was also once the home of the Fry's chocolate factory, later to be an offshoot of Cadbury Bournville, producing calorific delights such as Double Deckers, Mini Eggs, and Crunchie. Sadly they are no more, new masters Kraft closing the factory that was built in 1923 and shifting production to a new factory in Poland. And there was I thinking that all the Poles were over here working as plumbers in Southampton. Silly me.

Not too much for Keynsham to boast about now you may think, but they can still point proudly to the fact that Marcus Trescothick, the Somerset and England cricketer, was born there, as was comedian and entertainer, Bill Bailey. But it does beg the question doesn't it? If Keynsham was such a great place, why is the age-old question always being asked: 'Bill Bailey won't you please come home?' He should already be a resident there.

Weather conditions were good as we continued west towards Bristol; mild temperatures and little wind, and we were soon at the ring road of the city. Even better, there was an official cycle path that took us away from the busy Bank Holiday Monday traffic.

The Asda superstore at Hanham loomed up and Thomas made a strong case for a lunch stop. Personally I would have continued and survived on Jaffa bars and Kendal Mint Cake but, in all honesty, I didn't take much persuading.

The 45-minute break probably did both of us good after being tested by the abnormally long and arduous drags up the many miscellaneous and nondescript lanes south of Keynsham, so we locked our cycles and wandered in.

Even though we were dressed a little differently to the rest of the shoppers I had the uneasy feeling that we shouldn't have been there. For some ridiculous reason I felt as though we were gatecrashing a store celebrating a fat persons' convention. Pretty well without exception all the patrons were absolutely enormous. It was like a remake of the Incredible Hulk; men, woman and children alike all bursting out of their clothes.

I have never seen hands move so fast, stuffing their faces with pizzas and cakes, sometimes simultaneously. That is when the day's special offer of a chicken curry with chips wasn't being shifted. Boy, would I like to see a list of the top selling products in that particular store.

Can you imagine a shelf stacker's conversation with a customer?

'What was that you said, tomatoes, lettuce, cucumber? Now what's some of them then my lovely? We've got a nice line in pies. Got a special offer on doughnuts too.'

We ate up and left, slightly embarrassed that we had definitely been 'non-league' in the eating stakes compared to our west country diners.

For the next hour we enjoyed the relaxation of the cycle path, gently cruising through parkland and underpasses until we found ourselves in Fishponds. Problem was, we didn't want to be in Fishponds.

In a gentle and courteous manner, Thomas told me to put my map away and keyed into some gizmo on his mobile telephone. Through satellite coverage it pinpointed exactly where we were and, more importantly , where we wanted to be. Irritatingly it meant us retracing our steps for half an hour, a sure sign of failure, but it wasn't long before we were passing over the M32 and then the M5 motorways and sailing through Olveston and on to Aust and the services that overlook the River Severn.

Our Asda lunch stop and unplanned detour into Fishponds had cost us almost two hours and I was conscious that we had another 30 miles to travel, still a challenge as it was now way past four in the afternoon and we had yet to cross from England into Wales..

The old Severn Bridge, where we were crossing, was built as late as 1966, the main artery until then from South Wales to London being the A48 and A40 through Lydney, Gloucester Cheltenham and Oxford.

I can distinctly remember as a kid of five, when staying at my

Granny's house on the A40 in Charlton Kings just outside Cheltenham, watching car headlight beams race over the bedroom ceiling when I was lying in bed. In those days cars would pass every six or seven minutes. Can you believe the relatively sparse amount of traffic on the main thoroughfare between England and Wales as recent as 1950?

A further example of how times have changed is when you consider the cost of building the bridge. Just £8 m for a structure that took five years to erect, with two steel towers and 18,000 miles of wire. That's an awful lot of wire, enough to get to Bangkok and back and still have sufficient for a quick return hop to New York. To my mind it seems a superb investment, especially as the toll fees probably pushed it into profit within, I guess, about 15 years.

When the second Severn Bridge was built 30 years later, it cost a cool £300 m but only took four years to construct. In fairness, though, inflation has risen by almost 400 per cent, but it does make you think, doesn't it?

Thomas and I had the ritual photographs with the bridge as a backdrop, taken by a family who had walked over from the other side. The two young boys with their parents seemed contented enough, presumably happy that they had had the briefest of holidays in another country. That's if you can count a cup of tea and a bun in the Severn View Services on the M48 a holiday. I suppose it still beats Barry Island and Porthcawl hands down.

The slope off the cycle lane leaving the bridge heading towards Chepstow was quite a slog, and Thomas was beginning to feel the pace. Regardless of him being 22 and fit and healthy from year-round football and cricket, he was quickly realising that there is no substitute for getting cycling miles in your legs other than, well, cycling.

He doesn't come up short on guts though and although we had covered well over 60 miles, by the time we passed Chepstow racecourse he battled on without complaint, even if it was 50 yards behind his Dad.

It really came home to me the benefit of all the training I had done since the previous November, both on the exercise bike and out on the road. In spite of cycling 200 miles in the last three days, most of them feeling as though they were uphill, we had a situation where a man three times his son's age was having to cajole and encourage him to complete the last few miles of the day. I don't say this in a superior, 'holier than thou' way at all, just to emphasise how important it is to prepare properly for a cycling challenge.

We followed the A466 that runs alongside the River Wye away from Chepstow for the 16 miles to Monmouth, at the midway point passing Tintern Abbey, a ruin now but the home of Cistercian monks as far back as 1131. Quite frankly, Thomas couldn't have cared if it had been circumcised monkeys dating back to 24BC as, by now, he was well and truly out on his feet, or to put it more bluntly and accurately, out on his wheels.

But, he wouldn't give in and I will always remember with great fatherly pride how, when old ladies of 90 years plus walked past him with their Zimmer frames as he rode along, telling him that he could do it and to keep going, he smiled back at them and never once felt inclined to tell them to stuff their walking Zimmers in a place where no man had gone before. Well not for a considerable time anyway. That's pure class.

We eventually arrived in Monmouth where I left Thomas outside the Lidl supermarket for his mother to collect him and bring him up to my next B&B stop at Hillersland, a little village just north of Coleford. OK, I cheated a bit too, I left my panniers with him.

Climbing out of Monmouth and away from the Wye, on the A4136, was an absolute joy. It was steep and meandered up through the outer reaches of the Forest of Dean, but without my weighty panniers it seemed so simple, I felt I was flying. For those few magical moments I could have ridden on for a further 50 miles, it was a wonderful feeling of power. Similar to my ride into Taunton the previous day, I felt I was getting to grips with this epic journey I was on.

Halfway up I passed Christine and her friend, Janice, coming down so I knew Thomas would not have long to wait for his own personal broom wagon.

At the top of the long climb I was expecting a sign for Hillersland, but after clearing Staunton I could not find one, just directions to Coleford and Berry Hill. Fortunately there was a local man strolling towards me so I stopped to ask for directions. The conversation went something like this.

'Excuse me, can you tell me the way to Hillersland please?'

'Yeah, sure can my son, no problems there. You goes back the way you come, till you sees a white building, well more grey really, but it was white once like. Turn right there, you can't turn left so go right, then straight through Christchurch and it's another mile after that. If you gets to Symonds Yat don't you worry, don't you worry at all, just turn round and come back 'cause you've missed it. Now, tell me again, where did you want to get to?'

Quite unbelievable, but hey, I had only been on my bike for over seven hours and covered close on 80 miles, why should I pass judgement?

The last time I met a 'Forester' was when I was about 15 and playing football for Charlton Kings in the North Gloucestershire Senior League at places like Cinderford, Lydbrook and Bream, all deep in the Forest of Dean. Then, a Forester's idea of fun was extracting as much blood as possible from your legs in 90 minutes, with double points if bones were broken too. A strange breed when it comes to enjoying sporting pastimes.

I thanked my guide for his expertise and began to move off. He winked, smiled, shrugged his shoulder in a Del Boy-like manner and left me with: 'All right my son?'

I'm sure he was trying his best but he hadn't filled me with confidence. In fact I was seriously contemplating riding back to Chepstow, over the Severn Bridge and taking the busy A38 up through Gloucester and coming in from another angle.

At quarter to eight that evening, I eventually rode into Hillersland where my family were waiting. My host Chris Lathan's accommodation was first-class, more motel than B&B, with a single-storey block alongside his main house containing several large and attractively appointed rooms. The breakfast room turned out to be equally as impressive with every conceivable breakfast item you could wish for. Not the cheapest place I stayed in but still great value.

Within 10 minutes I was showered and changed and ready for the family reunion over dinner. Chris recommended the New Inn, a pub restaurant in the next village, so we hurried off to try to beat last food orders. That mission was accomplished, although at that late hour on a Bank Holiday Monday it was quicker to ask: 'What have you got?' than order from the menu.

The highlight of the evening though was not the food, although that was fine, or the excellent beer. No, it was the owner of the pub, a wizened old Irishman called Jack Leahy, who I would guess was well into his 70s.

Photographs of Jack at race meetings at Kempton, Ludlow, Cheltenham, plus many more courses adorned the pub walls, usually with him stood in the paddock, next to a horse and jockey. Frequently he was holding a large winner's trophy. He was clearly an owner and indisputably a character.

He came over to our table and I said, showing great observational skills, 'So, you're a racing man Jack?' Not the most searching of statements but it got the show on the road.

Jack pulled up a chair and was off, telling us about the various horses he had owned, the trophies that he had won, the meetings he had attended, all his sentences being sprinkled liberally with 'feckin' this and 'feckin' that. He really was a walking cabaret. His best line was in answer to my question on whether his wife accompanied him racing.

'Don't ask,' he said, 'I once persuaded her to come to a race meeting with me by buying her a new coat. She came into the paddock with me to see my horse, patted it on the nose and it bit the "feckin" sleeve off her "feckin" new coat. She never came again.'

Sadly at 11 p.m. it was time to say goodbye to Jack, say farewell to Christine, her friend Janice, and son Thomas who were returning to Oxfordshire and leaving me to get a good night's sleep before continuing on my way north.

As I lay in bed that night I felt sorry for my family having to take the 90-minute car journey home while I was tucked up warm. I appreciated the effort that they had made coming to see me and giving me encouragement to finish the ride. Most of all I had loved the time I had spent on the road with Thomas. Magical moments.

But as well as my thoughts for the family my mind constantly wandered back to our genial host, Jack Leahy in the New Inn and his virtuoso performance over dinner. What a 'feckin' character.

I slept well.

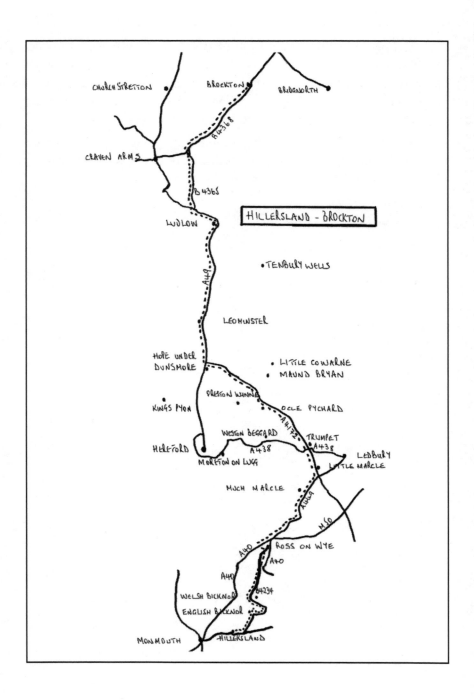

HILLERSLAND - BROCKTON

Day 5
Hillersland to Brockton

PROMTPLY at 9 a.m., in miserable drizzle, following an overnight deluge, I left Hillersland and immediately disappeared into a tight narrow lane that descended the two miles to the B4234 that would carry me though to Ross-on-Wye.

The politically correct named villages of English Bicknor and Welsh Bicknor came and went , and I was managing to maintain a steady 14 mph, made all the easier after discarding my waterproof trousers. I had always had a problem with them, finding them restrictive and a terrible distraction with their 'swish swish' noise every time I turned a pedal.

I was soon in Ross-on-Wye, a small market town of around 10,000 inhabitants, which nestles deep in south-east Herefordshire.

Being a relatively small place I quickly found myself right in the middle of the town, surrounded by centuries-old grand buildings, now spoiled by the multicoloured street level fascias of the usual motley crew of national retailers that are now past masters in defacing pretty well every High Street in the country. I remembered that Lavenham in Suffolk was still one of the few exceptions, a small town that violently objects to this behaviour. Long may they hold that stance.

From Ross I needed to find the A449 that would take me north-east for a short while, then the A4172 that would carry me north-west, up into Leominster.

Instead of figuring out what was a simple map reading exercise , I foolishly asked one of the town's senior citizens if he could apply a little local knowledge.

In the short time since leaving Land's End I had grown accustomed to locals, when asked to give directions, half closing their eyes and sucking air in through clenched teeth, instantly giving the impression that it wasn't a particularly good idea to start from that position. Try it and you will see what I mean. This one didn't disappoint, and I instinctively knew I was in trouble.

He sent me over a beautiful old stone bridge crossing the Wye and down to a busy roundabout that had slightly more traffic circling it than Piccadilly Circus in the rush hour. It was the A40 that comes up from Newport before joining the M50, the main transport artery between South Wales, the Midlands and the North. It became instantly clear to me that the Midlands and the North were in dire need of supplies, as the volume of freight lorries had to be seen to be believed. Not only was the bypass round Ross astonishingly busy it was also under at least an inch of water due to the overnight storm.

However, I had to take it and silently prayed that the three miles until the M50 and me turning on to the quieter A449 would pass quickly.

During the climb up a long gradient of the bypass the transport drivers had enormous fun with me, and it soon became clear to me that there was a game that the drivers played with helpless cyclists following any rainfall. It was perfect weather to induct me into their game.

The game was probably called 'Soak the Cyclist' and been devised in some 'Greasy Spoon' on the A1 many years earlier. It had very simple rules.

The winner would be the driver that drove closest to any unprotected cyclist, with additional points given based on the quantity of water that they could spray from their tyres on to the helpless victim. If there was a tie, the overall winner would be decided on the volume of spray emitted after they had passed. So, in simple terms, it was wobble, splash and spray.

Well, they did have fun didn't they? They were bloody competitive too, with everyone wanting to win. I bet they couldn't wait to pull in at Strensham Services on the M5, compare notes and have a good laugh about their wheeze.

If I had been judging I would have voted for the Tesco HGV, just edging out Eddie Stobart after a tiebreak, with a Pickfords removal van coming a rather distant third. I'll tell you, that Tesco man was good, certainly giving me a 'two for the price of one' deal via his multitude of tyres.

Not only was I drenched to the skin and mentally scarred for life, I was rendered blind. Oil from the road mixed with the spray formed a deadly and painful concoction. I fully accepted that I was going to die from lead poisoning, but was equally keen to be able to see clearly when that moment arrived; sadly it looked as though I would be sightless first.

The stinging from my eyes was astonishingly painful but not quite painful enough to prevent me from disqualifying a Norbert Dentressangle wagon AND trailer after I spotted him coming up behind me for the third time in less than a mile. Absolute proof in my eyes, well what remained of them, that you can never trust a Johnny Foreigner to play fair.

While there were major downsides to my experience on the bypass, like life, there were invariably upsides to each problem. I found one. The oil that was causing me pain acted as a great lubricant for my eyes for the remainder of my ride, and I can honestly report that it was well over seven weeks before my eyes squeaked when I blinked.

Off the Ross bypass and free from being the stooge in the Aquatic Splash Down Championships for vehicles of 40 tonnes and over, I headed on to the quieter A449 and was able to reflect on my journey to date.

While only being on the road for just over four days I had already experienced the highs and lows of long distance cycling; the joys of being free from the pressures of every day life; the chance to appreciate the beautiful countryside that lay around me, much of it missed when travelling by car; and the kind and warm hearted people who had helped me. I also reminded myself of the great characters that would give me my material when I relayed the story of my ride to anyone daft enough to listen.

Each county had been different in its own way. The rugged unspoilt beauty of Cornwall, the staggering hills that I encountered in Devon, the flatter lands of Somerset south of the Mendips and the unforgettable ride along the Bridgwater and Taunton canal.

Add to that the briefest of glimpses of the county where I was born, Gloucestershire, before crossing the old Severn Bridge into Wales and the magical meandering ride following the River Wye up through Monmouthshire. So much in just 4 days, I could already return home contented.

But, of course, there were also flip sides to my journey. The high-speed crash on the second day was a setback, more so because I was travelling alone. My inability to accurately read the Cycling Touring Club directions and marry them to my map was another difficulty I had to improve upon; my problem not theirs I hasten to add. And the rigid schedule I had set myself, regardless of circumstance – always having to reach my pre-booked B&B accommodation by the end of each day. Already I was realising that I could have ridden longer on some of the legs, even if it was only another 20 odd miles or so.

But all in all I was happy with my performance to date and knew that the next three days would be across flatter terrain compared to the ground I had already travelled over since the start. The might of the Scottish Highlands were still some way off and there would be plenty of time to worry about them when I reached the border.

To boost my morale, the good people of Herefordshire were also acknowledging my epic ride and taking me to their hearts by placing bunting and St Georges flags, not only on their cars but also on the garden fences and bedroom windows of their homes. It was a wonderful gesture from folk who I had never met and never would meet, and it greatly helped my morale as I continued on my lonely ride north. The red and white flags were truly patriotic and touched me greatly and I sincerely hoped that, after I had passed by, they would not take them down until after the Soccer World Cup in South Africa had finished in a few weeks' time!

I was quickly becoming addicted to the weirdly wonderful names of the surrounding villages. They fascinated me and helped pass the time on the more mundane sections. Every crossroads was an opportunity for me to indulge myself, read the place name and imagine how they acquired the name. Herefordshire was right up there with the best.

I saw signposts introducing me to off-the-wall places such as Ocle Pychard, Preston Wynne, Little Cowarne, Moreton-on-Lugg, Weston Beggard, Kings Pyon, Maund Bryan, plus so many more. They were names that were impossible to make up, but somehow somebody had. I would love to have attended some of those early Parish Council meetings.

Two of the early villages that I had heard of soon after leaving Ross on Wye were Little Marcle and Much Marcle, the latter the original home of mass murderer Fred West before he moved to Gloucester to carry out his atrocities. Rumours are rife about how he was introduced to sex by his mother, but I don't believe them for one minute. However, it did strike me as a shade odd that all the children I saw looked very similar to each other. How does that happen?

Wet and bedraggled from the incessant drizzle, I decided to stop for coffee after spotting a Texaco garage-cum-minimart service station. It was a welcome sight as I crossed the A438 east of Hereford, and being situated close to the village of Trumpet thought it rude if I didn't pop in for a bit of a blow out.

I locked my bike to one of those stands that sells potted plants, thinking that if my bike is stolen I would soon find it by leafing through the latest edition of 'Herefordshire's Best Kept Gardens'. The next task was emptying my cycling shoes of water before I strode purposefully into the shop with my two panniers. I suspected the worst when the young girl on the till said: 'What pump please?'

Picture the scene if you would: a black cycling helmet, yellow hi-vis rain jacket, Lycra shorts, cycling gloves, shoes with cleats and two panniers.

Oh how I wanted to respond: 'Number four please and also four litres of engine oil and a fan belt for a Vauxhall Astra.'

But you don't do you? You let the moment pass with a knowing smile. She was young and still probably hadn't crossed the border of her beloved county.

Instead I asked for a large white coffee followed by a muffin and even that set her off into a fit of giggles. Honestly some people. What's so funny about that?

I took my refreshments but found it difficult to manoeuvre round the mini market with refreshments and two panniers, so edged to the other end of the counter where I saw what I took to be the Manageress.

My, was she a big woman, an absolute Goliath.

It looked as though her tabard had been tailored from the big top of Billy Smart's circus with a further bit borrowed from Bertram Mills to finish the piping. On the top of her head her hair was slightly singed from standing under one of the ceiling lights. Honestly, she was that tall.

'Is there anywhere I can stuff these panniers please?' I said.

She stared at me, said nothing but we both knew immediately that we were thinking of the same place, even if we disagreed on the recipient. Fortunately the young girl who had offered me a muffin interjected and they were safely stored behind the counter while I wandered round the shop.

Now, there is only so much time one can spend at a newspaper stand in a mini market before it is clear that news is being extracted without any intention of a purchase so, still with my coffee and cake, I moved on to the food area to peruse the wares.

Immediately I saw that Lloyd Grossman's tomato and basil bolognaise sauce was badly overpriced at £3.79 for 350 grams especially as Dolmio, for a similar cost, offered 500 grams.

'Come on Lloyd, play the game,' I thought. You're not in a celebrity's house filming a 'Through the Keyhole' TV programme now, handing back to David Frost in that strangled Boston accent: 'Back to you David.' Your name is on the jar of bolognaise sauce and it is costing some poor

Trumpeter a small fortune.

Even worse was the price of 99p for a basic can of Heinz baked beans. Goodness only knows what the cost would have been had a few midget sausages been swimming around in them. Worse still if old Lloyd had muscled in with his name on the tin.

It was obvious to me that there was either a lot of money floating about in this neck of the woods, shoppers were not particularly attentive, or the grasping tentacles of Tesco, Sainsbury's and Morrisons had yet to erect anything vaguely close to the parish of Trumpet, Herefordshire.

I finished my coffee, flicked the remaining muffin crumbs from my chin deftly into the ripe plums in the fruit and veg, collected my panniers and made my way out of the shop.

Before me was a sight for sore eyes. Lying flat on her back in the oil and grime of the forecourt was Goliath, her arm down a manhole, trying to connect the nozzle of a fuel tanker's pipe to the underground store. Our eyes met, I smiled and waved my two panniers to and fro. She remained motionless. We both knew who the winner was in our little encounter; the fight was over and lessons hopefully learned.

Don't mess with bike man when he's enjoying a muffin.

At Hope-under-Dinmore I rode past the main gate of Hampton Court Castle, its history dating back to before the 15th century. I made a mental note to learn more about the estate when I returned home, not that I am particularly knowledgeable about history; I'm not old enough.

It appears that Henry IV granted permission to merge two manors into one. I suppose in many respects it was rather like the notorious Kray twins in the 60s, merging the 'manors' of Bethnall Green and Stepney.

Anyway, I can only think that one of the owners, John Arkwright, who lived there in Hampton Court castle in the 1860s must have fallen on hard times, as I can distinctly remember watching a TV programme with him running a corner shop up North together with a very young David Jason. I assume it is the same bloke anyway, although he did look a bit like Ronnie Barker. Maybe my history isn't so bad after all.

The A49 was relatively flat and I made good time to Leominster, a town with a population slightly larger than Ross and second only to Hereford in the whole county.

Plenty of black and white wooden framed houses gave me the impression that the town was an interesting one to browse in but I had other ideas, I was only halfway to my destination in Brockton and an evening with my old Derby County footballing colleagues, Alan Durban and Ritchie Barker.

Much later, when idly 'Googling' my way up my ride, I noted that Albert Lees, one of the World's foremost pop guitarists was born in Leominster. Two more of Albert's many claims to fame was playing in Bill Wyman's Rhythm Kings and once being the boyfriend of my wife's best friend's mother. How's that for reflected glory?

It is my firm view that Wikipedia rather harshly summed up Leominster by listing under its 'Local Attractions' – a chip shop.

No wonder Albert dedicated his early years to guitar lessons in order to move out and mingle with the pop music elite in London to achieve fame and fortune. For Albert, the cod in batter just didn't appeal.

It wasn't long before Ludlow came into view, but instead of going into town I followed the ring road that ascends the long but not difficult climb round to the east.

I know Ludlow quite well from my travel days when I regularly used to visit the Ellerman Travel shop that was based in the town. It was rumoured that the Manager of the shop lived in a caravan with no sanitation, his personal hygiene providing proof that was difficult to argue against. He must have been nearing 70 when he eventually stood down but not before he had created a name for himself in the vicinity for being the undisputed expert on outdoor holidays. You can't beat personal experience I suppose. A case of been there, done it, got the dirty t-shirt.

North of Ludlow I moved on to the B4365 that took me across Ludlow racecourse. The ground inside the rails is reserved for Ludlow Golf Club, and, with no race meeting on that day, only golfers were out in force.

The riding was easy and the weather had improved considerably, a warm early afternoon sun having taken over from the morning's drizzle.

It was a quiet road and I let my mind wander over the possible public address messages that could be relayed to punters as they stood in the main stand watching the steeplechasing on race days.

'I regret to announce that it has been necessary to abandon the 2.15 halfway through the race due to a jockey being lost in the rough near the 6th fairway. There is also a horse loose on the course after refusing the par 3 5th. Finally the 2.45 will not get under way until Major Montague-Smythe, our generous patron, has taken his ninth putt on the 18th and made his way to the weigh-in room. Thank you'.

A few miles from the racecourse the B4365 merged with the B4368 coming up from Craven Arms and I was now only about 14 undulating miles from Brockton and my next night's accommodation. However, as I had already found out, the last few miles are always the longest, the mind seemingly closing down early under the assumption that work is finished for the day.

The last five miles seemed like an eternity not helped by being harassed by a motorised stalker. I had read about young girls being followed through the streets by dirty old men in macs, but this was the first time to my knowledge that a man a few months off drawing his old age pension had been hassled by the mysterious owner of a silver Peugeot.

I first noticed the car when it passed me going in the other direction. But within five minutes it had turned round and was back cruising slowly by me at a sedate 18 mph.

I refused to be intimidated or make eye contact, although I realised I was in a pretty dangerous situation out in the wilds of Shropshire. He could be armed or even have a large weapon that could cause me pain.

He stopped about 50 yards in front of me and I could feel his eyes boring into me as I rode closer. I overtook him, my gaze never leaving the road a few feet in front of my wheel, while at the same time trying to look as masculine as a man could in Lycra cycling gear. My face was now

75

set in a fierce grimace as I increased my pace by an extra 3 miles an hour. I was not going to be easy pickings for anybody.

I glanced back and saw that he was on the move again, edging closer to my back wheel. Oh my God, I thought, here I am, mid afternoon on a deserted B road and I've got a bloody maniac behind me wanting my body – perhaps more.

He trailed me for the last mile into Brockton, tantalising and teasing me by revving his engine in throaty roars. It sounded to me as though he had somehow trained his car to make erotic noises to compliment his own perverted desires.

A lunatic and a motor with a red-hot exhaust pipe. When and how would it end?

Boy, was I in trouble. Even the muffin was now causing me heartburn. How ironic.

I have never been happier than I was when the Brockton sign came in to view and I was able to grind to a halt outside the Feathers pub/restaurant in the centre of the village.

I wheeled round to face my stalker, at the same time feeling for my mobile phone in order to call my landlady, Tricia Webb and seek directions to her Old Quarry Cottage home where I would be safe.

The car had stopped 30 yards back and was now flashing its headlights on and off, possibly the last dice the car had been trained to throw in an effort to woo me. I pretended to adjust something on my front wheel but heard the sound of the driver's door slamming and the noise of his shoes across the gravel as he came towards me. He spoke for the first time.

'All right boyo, you made good time up that last hill, you went quicker than I thought'.

I looked up to be confronted by Alan Durban, my good friend from my days at Derby County who had agreed to meet me at the end of my day's ride. Alan played 350 games for the club and under Brian Clough's management helped them win the 1st Division (now the Premier League) in 1971-72. He also played 27 times for Wales as well as being granted the highest accolade by Derby fans, being voted in to their all-time team of Derby County legends.

As much as I admired and respected Alan all I could muster in the way of a welcome was: 'Twat'.

After leaving my bike at my B&B I jumped in with Alan and we drove to Ironbridge, where Alan gave me a brief history of the town.

It's a village on the River Severn at the heart of the Ironbridge Gorge and famous for its 30 metre bridge built by Abraham Darby III in 1779. As I sat being photographed overlooking the famous bridge I could not help musing over the amazing coincidence.

How the first iron bridge ever constructed was erected in a town called Ironbridge. Just goes to show that truth is stranger than fiction eh?

In the evening we were joined by Ritchie Barker, another old colleague from my Baseball Ground days, who also had a long football career with Notts County and Peterborough before going in to football management. Together with their partners Jane and Liz we enjoyed a very pleasant dinner at a restaurant near Alan's home.

The girls talked mainly about Liz's forthcoming gig (she's a jazz singer) at the Ascot race meeting a few days ahead while I received a revised routeing for the following day.

Alan is not one to worry too much about the expertise of the Cycling Touring Club, or the AA for that matter as he knows best. Confidence and plain speaking are never far from the surface with Al, regardless of the subject.

He is not a bad stalker either!

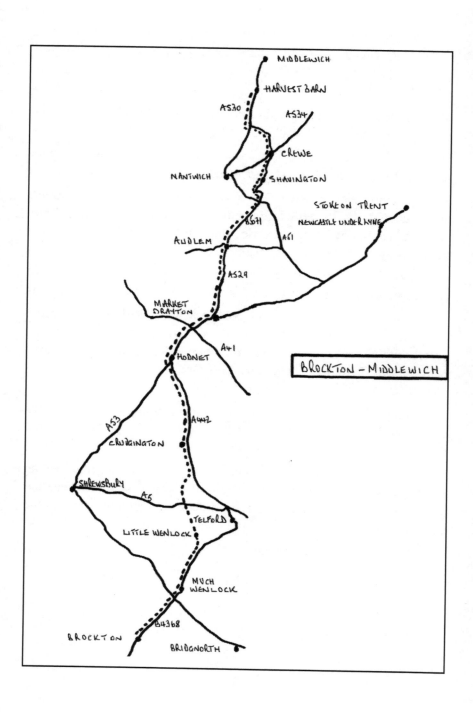

MIDDLEWICH

HARVEST BARN

A530

A534

CREWE

NANTWICH

SHAVINGTON

STOKE ON TRENT

NEWCASTLE UNDER LYNE

B671

A51

AUDLEM

A529

MARKET DRAYTON

A41

HODNET

A53

A442

CRUDGINGTON

SHREWSBURY

A5

TELFORD

LITTLE WENLOCK

MUCH WENLOCK

B4368

BROCKTON

BRIDGNORTH

BROCKTON - MIDDLEWICH

Day 6
Brockton to Middlewich

BEFORE starting my journey I shared breakfast with an artist from Liverpool who had been commissioned to paint some scenes around Much Wenlock. His perspective on life differed greatly from mine and I was so envious of the totally laid back way he viewed the world. With his relaxed style and the leisurely way he was painting his way through life I was confident he would not be lining the pockets of too many stress counsellors or psychiatrists in his later days.

Leaving Brockton, I was soon into my first climb of the day but the weather was again near perfect, with overcast skies forecast to change into a warm and sunny day.

I was only travelling 56 miles to Middlewich, just north of Crewe, a ridiculously short distance across the flat Cheshire plains. Based on the experience I had gained from my time on the road I was kicking myself that my day's target was such a short distance away.

When planning my overnight stays using the Cycling Touring Club accommodation guide I had experienced difficulty finding a suitable B&B closer to the Greater Manchester area and, being a novice, was not sure how I would be feeling physically after a full five days on the road. Looking back, in hindsight , I could have easily added another 30 miles to the day. I consoled myself with the view that it wasn't a race and today I could relax.

Within 20 minutes I was riding through Much Wenlock, a little known place to the great majority, but a town well known to Olympic historians. Few people know that there was a gap between the original Ancient games held in Olympia, Greece, every 4 years between 776BC and 337AD and the now modern Olympic movement.

Where does Much Wenlock fit into all this?

Well, in the mid 19th century a Doctor William Penny Brookes originated the Wenlock Olympic games before meeting Baron Pierre de Coubertin in the Raven Hotel in the town. The hotel still contains many Olympic artefacts from those early years and from their meeting. The games as we know them today was born.

Can you imagine, from humble beginnings in a small Shropshire village in 1866, the modern Olympic games began; a games that now stops the world every 4 years and brings together the elite athletes of the planet. My heart goes out to poor old Brookes. Everyone has heard of Pierre de Coubertin who is famed for the Olympic movement, but lets set the records straight: without Doctor Billy Brookes's foresight Sir Steven Redgrave could possibly be paddling a rowing boat on the Serpent every summer Sunday afternoon at a cost of £20.00 an hour.

It's pleasing to know that the two mascots for the 2012 London games are named Mandeville and Wenlock, a respectful nod to the great work undertaken at Stoke Mandeville hospital in Buckinghamshire as well as the foresight and energy of William Penny Brookes nearly 150 years ago.

Skirting the west side of Telford I continued north to my first rest stop in Crudgington. The previous evening, over dinner, Alan had promised to meet me with a welcoming cup of tea and a few fingers of Kit-Kat before hurrying off for his beloved game of golf at his club in Oswestry.

I reluctantly agreed but only after gaining his commitment that he would stay in a pre-agreed meeting place as I still had mental scars from the previous day. In seriousness it was a kind gesture from Alan and one that I appreciated even if it was shortened by his instructions to get the final two fingers of my snack down a bit smartish, as he was due on the first tee in under an hour.

From Crudgington I ventured on to the A442 along the fast, flat, quiet roads of Shropshire through Hodnet and across the A41 towards Market Drayton.

The roads were peaceful, the weather ideal for cycling, just a fraction of breeze from the north but certainly nothing to impede my progress. The Wrekin countryside was truly at its best – it was another one of those perfect riding days. No pressure to eat up miles, no major hills, next to no traffic, no aches and pains to cause anguish, just a nice gentle run towards Middlewich. Except for a faint hint of loneliness, it was another sublime day.

Market Drayton soon came into view and my next geography lesson was immediately under way. The town has two major industries, one being the Kerry Group, the maker of sausages and other meat products under the Pork Farms and Asda labels. My mind raced back to my brief stay in the Asda store in the suburbs of Bristol. My those good souls from the district of Hanham would have been green with envy if they had known I was in the 'town of pies'.

To them a visit here would be like a Roman Catholic pilgrimage to Lourdes or maybe an Islamic trip to Mecca. My guess is that they would probably plump for Mecca until they were informed that it was the holy site in Saudi Arabia and not the local Bingo hall.

Muller Dairies, makers of Muller Lite, was the other main industry the town boasted, although a glance at the portly, red-faced pedestrians scurrying around in the late morning heat confirmed to me that they were keen Kerry fans in preference to Muller supporters.

It's possible, of course, that after working all day, up to their eyes in slimming food, the last thing they wanted when they got home was a carton of fruity non-fat cream. Stick another banger in the pan would be my cry too.

Before either industry became entwined with Market Drayton, Clive of India was the most famous name associated with the town, that is, if you ignore Oswald Mosley and Derek Podmore.

Derek, or as the local people named him, 'Poddy' Podmore, was a petty criminal, well known by everyone in the town. Some would say he was a bloody nuisance, others a likeable old rogue. You pay your money and take your choice.

Folklore has it that at Christmas in 1977 he dressed up as Santa Claus and sat on the roof of Shrewsbury jail dispensing cigarettes and tobacco to the inmates below. His bellow of 'Merry Christmas' as he threw each handful of 'baccy' down probably made it a very festive scene.

Another of his stunts was to nail his ear to a tree, although it is unrecorded what happened next.

Other notable incidents that would have filled the local Tourist Board leaflets include appearing in court as a frogman and, at a separate hearing, covering himself in manure and wearing a dead pig on his head.

His *'raison d'être'* he saved for 1974, allegedly inventing the World live frog swallowing championships. He wasn't just the originator though – he was also the lead competitor, gracing the occasion with distinction by washing down each amphibian with a pint of black and tan.

So, hypothetically, if you had to choose who you would wish to spend a lively Friday night with, out and about in the pubs in Market Drayton, who would it be? Clive, Oswald or Poddy?

Give me Poddy every time as long as he doesn't follow me home.

Looking back, Market Drayton has a lot more going for it than I originally thought. Pies, yoghurt and frog swallowing, or put another way, meat, dairy produce and greens adds up to a pretty healthy diet.

I left town via the A529 ignoring my initial thoughts of taking B roads and lanes – the A roads in this part of the country were not busy, and I greedily ate up the miles on the flat roads crossing the Cheshire Plains.

Audlem came and went, and I avoided Nantwich by taking a more minor road cross-country to Crewe.

Just after leaving Audlem I was overtaken by two young riders moving at a faster speed than me. As I had already learned, the spirit of the road is for cyclists to slow down and have a brief chat before moving on, that is unless you are a more professional cyclist and travelling at the speed of light.

My new visitors had left Land's End on Saturday lunch-time compared to my Friday morning and were endeavouring to be at John O'Groats within 11 days, fully 4 days quicker than me. We exchanged tales and they pressed on leaving me to momentarily sulk that I was being a slow coach. My silly mood did not last for long, however, common sense soon telling me that the two lads were at least 40 years younger than me and were not carrying any weighty panniers. I even perked myself up by thinking 'whatever could have delayed them?'

As I rode on I wondered where my next highlight might be - something or somewhere to lift me, motivate and inspire me for the remainder of my ride.

Instead I rode into Crewe.

Ah, Crewe, of railway junction fame and the producer of Rolls-Royce cars and more latterly, Bentleys. In spite of my cynicism the town has quite a pedigree.

Every country needs a town like Crewe even in this computer driven age we live in. It's solid, proud to be working class and full of manufacturing companies both large and small. Each one employs people who don't mind getting a sweat on or dirtying their hands as they go about their business. I bet it has some great real ale too.

Much as I like Crewe and I really do, plus everything it stands for, with the best will in the world some of its inhabitants are not too easy on the eye.

Maybe I was unlucky to ride through the town in the early afternoon and not see the population at its best. On the other hand, with a strong desire to hunt down the Alexandra stadium, home to the local football team, maybe I wasn't as observant as I might have been.

My hunger to hunt down Crewe Alexandra FC was soon satisfied. It was easy to spot, the main stand rising high above the surrounding terraced houses, warehouses and factories.

Being a football nut I propped my bike against a lamp post in Gresty Road and took a few photographs of the ground. Not for me, castles, churches and statues - give me the main stand or entrance of any league football club and you will have one happy cyclist.

What could be better in my life? A beautiful summer's day, a cloudless sky, ahead of schedule and a photograph of the main stand of Crewe Alexandra Football Club. Life doesn't get much better than that – ever.

It was when I was cycling away from the ground towards town and the road to Middlewich, that it suddenly dawned on me.

I had been riding through Crewe for fully 30 minutes and I had not seen a male resident with a full head of hair. Let me be truthful here, I am excluding those who are naturally short of follicles, purely counting those whose lack of hair is self-inflicted. I racked my brains for a reason for this phenomenon, eventually arriving at two possible answers.

One, and this does not absolve recipients in any way, all hairdressers in Crewe could have a very serious attitude problem and two, it is entirely possible that a quite extraordinary outbreak of nits had descended upon to the town.

There could have been other reasons, but they escaped me, that is until the penny dropped.

Consider the evidence. Early afternoon, close to a league club's stadium and three months before the start of the 2010-11 football season.

Yep, easy isn't it. They had all been attending auditions for employment as football hooligans. I'd have taken them all, no arguments.

As I left the northern suburbs of the town behind me I passed the Leighton Hospital. The one and only time I had been there was about 35 years earlier, visiting Colin Boulton, a great friend of mine who was lying in bed nursing a broken leg sustained while playing for Lincoln City against the local club.

Colin was in the twilight of his career and his leg break speeded the end of his football life; sadly it was his final game. He didn't have a bad career though, playing 344 games for Derby County and the only player to be ever present in their two Football League Championship years (that is what they used to called the Premier League) in the 70s. He then went across to the States for a couple of 'golden hurrah' years in Tulsa and Los Angeles, before retiring from the game and taking up a sales position with Mitre Sports.

Speaking to him after my ride I told him I had ridden past the Leighton, and he swore blind that nobody visited him while he was there. Visit him? I made a 200-mile round trip to visit him. There's bloody gratitude for you. Belatedly he now says he was under sedation.

My night stop was midway between Crewe and Middlewich at the aptly named Harvest Barn in Wimboldsley. The Harvest Barn is not your average B&B but a refurbished barn with about six rooms above a farm shop which sells local produce such a real ale, cakes, potatoes, eggs, chicken and a whole lot more 'fair trade' food. Looking back it has to be one of my favourite stops.

As soon as I arrived I was invited to have tea and cakes in the café. A request for laundry quickly followed and when I enquired after the nearest restaurant for dinner not only was I offered a free taxi service to the two suggested but also, as an alternative, personal room service with pasta, pudding and real ale.

It would have been rude to refuse, and I spent a rather leisurely evening lying on the bed watching TV and reading while enjoying the wonderful fare that Trish Ryan provided. It was so sublime I actually felt guilty.

Breakfast the next morning matched the quality of the previous day's afternoon tea and dinner, and , together with my freshly laundered cycling gear, I think I got a pretty good bargain for the £40.00 I was charged.

Trish and her daughter Anne-Marie, plus Marjorie and Peter ,were truly exceptional and definitely lived up to the old adage in sales – exceed the customer's expectations and you have them for life.

I was now through day six of my ride and with very few exceptions, the major one being my altercation with a gravel lane in Cornwall, I was having a ball. In honesty it wasn't the fantastic scenery that was bringing me so much joy, it was the scores of wonderful people I was meeting en route. They were making my ride an absolute pleasure.

Where had they been hiding all my life?

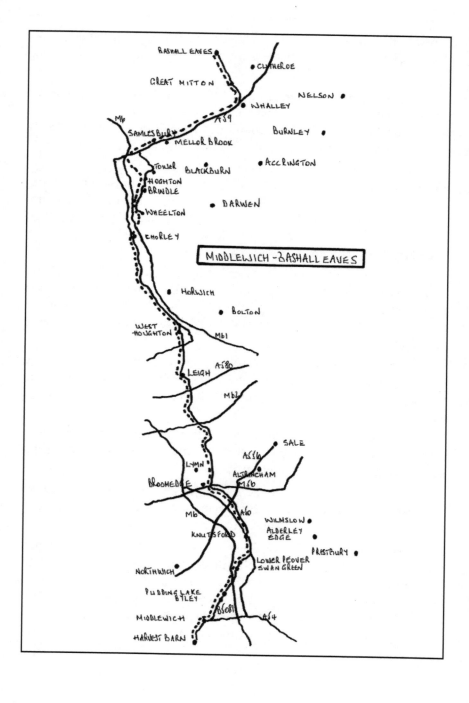

BASHALL EAVES

CLITHEROE

GREAT MITTON

NELSON

WHALLEY

A59

M6

BURNLEY

SAMLESBURY

MELLOR BROOK

ACCRINGTON

TOWER
BLACKBURN
HOGHTON
BRINDLE

DARWEN

WHEELTON

CHORLEY

MIDDLEWICH - BASHALL EAVES

HORWICH

BOLTON

WEST
HOUGHTON

M61

A580

LEIGH

M62

SALE

LYMN

A556

ALTRINCHAM

BROOMEDGE

M56

M6

A50

WILMSLOW

KNUTSFORD

ALDERLEY
EDGE

PRESTBURY

LOWER PEOVER
SWAN GREEN

NORTHWICH

PUDDINGLAKE
B'TLEY

MIDDLEWICH

B5081

A54

HARVEST BARN

Day 7
Middlewich to Bashall Eaves

DURING the preparation for my ride I had carefully evaluated each day's degree of difficulty, with, predominantly, mileage and terrain being my two main considerations.

Today was the stage that featured low down on my list of favourites, as it was the day that took me through densely built-up populated areas with plenty of heavy traffic.

Additionally, my map reading skills, or lack of them, would be stretched – it would be a severe test of my ability to remain heading in the right direction, that being broadly north.

Again the weather was kind to me – warm sunshine and a slight breeze welcoming me to the road following my prompt 08.30 departure from the Harvest Barn.

I was quickly through Middlewich and on to the quiet B5081 that wound through Byley and Puddinglake, then, up and over the M6 to Swan Green and Lower Peover.

During the early part of the day, I realised for the first time, just how far I had travelled. In a brief call to my wife I apologetically mentioned that I had ridden just 56 miles the previous day, only to be reminded that up until a week ago that would have been the second-longest ride of my life. After clocking up five consecutive days of 70 miles plus, the short distance appeared to be child's play – quite an improvement.

I also had visual proof that I was making progress, even if it was at a rather sedate speed of 12 miles an hour. Overhead in the clear blue sky was a procession of aircraft flying, maybe at 2,000 ft, either making their approach or taking their departure from Manchester Airport. Ridiculous as it may seem for a man who had spent a good part of his life driving the highways and byways of England it dawned on me that Manchester was in the north of the country, and I had actually ridden there by bike.

Travelling through Lower Peover a few miles south of Knutsford I suddenly felt queasy and dizzy, and I began to hallucinate. I was confused. I had not travelled for much more than an hour, the sun had yet to reach its zenith, so what was the problem? Surely I wasn't dehydrated – I had taken plenty of sips from my energy drink bottle.

Yet the symptoms were all there as I rode through Lower Peover village. I began to see strange things. It was if my imagination was running wild. The Queen was sitting on top of a hedge, Charlie Chaplin was leaning against a tree, a pink pig, wearing little girls' clothes, was sitting astride a farm gate. There were many more instances. My sight and mind were playing tricks on me.

Fortunately I spotted a man in his garden and stopped to seek help, but when I called to him he ran into his house, never to be seen again. I gulped down more liquid and tried to stay calm but the whole situation was getting ridiculous. I still had 60 miles to ride and I was already struggling.

With the village a ghost town and images still flashing before my eyes, I rode on quickly and soon hit the outskirts of Knutsford. Fortunately the odd characters I had seen had now disappeared, and I was beginning to feel myself again – even though I knew that it was a dirty and dangerous habit to have when riding a bike.

But I couldn't erase the Queen, Charlie and Miss Piggy from my thoughts, so stopped at an Esso garage and explained my dilemma to the female sales assistant on the till.

She smiled softly at me.

'Silly you,' she said. 'It's something the villagers do every May Bank Holiday. They make life-sized characters and have a competition, the winner being the one that is most life-like. It's a tradition pet.'

Bloody tradition I thought, not when it scares the shit out of a cyclist trying to get from one end of Britain to another. There ought to be a law against it. At the very least there should be signs displayed stating:

'IF YOU ARE RIDING FROM LAND'S END TO JOHN O'GROATS ON JUNE 3RD AND SEE A MEMBER OF THE MONARCHY, A FILM STAR OR AN ANIMAL DRESSED IN WOMEN'S CLOTHING LOUNGING AROUND THIS VILLAGE, DON'T BE ALARMED BECAUSE WE ARE ALL MENTAL HERE AND LIKE TO PLAY SILLY GAMES'

Maybe not quite so specifically directed towards me, but you get my drift don't you?

Could have been worse though, the previous year a local resident made a model of a traffic policeman complete with speed radar gun – all the villagers came out to play for that one, watching the traffic slow almost to a halt. Rumour has it that the Chief Constable of Cheshire picked up a speeding ticket.

My brief glimpse of Knutsford confirmed to me what I had read in the newspapers - along with Prestbury and Alderley Edge, Knutsford is known as the 'golden triangle' and THE place to live in the North-West. It's home for stockbrokers and famous footballers and with property reputed to be the most expensive in the land other than the South-East and London, it wasn't difficult to see why.

Every house looked to be worth well in excess of £3 m and appeared to have its own personal gardener, the beautifully manicured grounds confirming that they were receiving slightly more attention than a quick whip round with the Flymo every Sunday morning.

A toiling gardener told me that Phil Jagielka and Bobby Charlton had their homes in the area, as did Nick Freeman, celebrity solicitor for the stars – Colin Montgomery and Sir Alex Ferguson being two to benefit from his excellent legal skills. In fact he drove past us as we chatted, but there was no chance he would be required by me to fight a speeding charge.

Tatton Park lies slightly to the north-east of the town and was the next highlight of the day. As Cheshire's leading tourist attraction and owned by the National Trust, it receives over 750,000 visitors a year and it is not difficult to see why. Even from the road it looked immaculate but, like so many places on my journey north, it would have to wait for another occasion; I still had many hard miles to go.

Continuing on lanes suggested by the CTC I crossed the A556 and officially moved from Cheshire into Greater Manchester, heading through Broomedge, a small village situated close to the M56. It was still not 10.30, yet I seemed to be making good progress on roads that hardly changed from the perfect horizontal.

Cycling completely alone is an interesting occupation, I don't mean for the odd training ride but for day after day after day. Admittedly I had enjoyed Thomas's company for a while, but I was now into my third day since he departed, and I had time to consider exactly what went through my mind for six to seven hours at a stretch.

It's a bit embarrassing to say, but the answer is, not a lot.

Sure, there is the passing countryside to look at, but even that gets to look the same after a bit. I defy anyone to be able to tell the difference between a field with cows in, in Shropshire and, say, a field with cows in, in Somerset. They're both greenish and the animals in both of them all go moo. No discernible accent either. So with the exception of the odd highlight, such as the coast, a lake, a hill, or a bridge the countryside forms an attractive, but somewhat standard, unchanging backdrop.

As already mentioned, the place names of villages are always good value, especially when you imagine what it is like for people who reside in them trying to explain to others where they live.

'Sorry, I didn't catch the name of the village you live in?'

'Um, I live in a little place called Wyre Piddle.'

'Pardon?'

'WYRE PIDDLE.'

If you are ever bored get hold of an atlas and take a look through it, you will have hours of endless fun. Oh believe me, in England and Scotland alone there are some real howlers.

ALLANSTANK – ARNY BAGS – BACKSIDE – BADGERS MOUNT – BEDLAM BOTTOM – BEGGARS BUSH – BELLYSIDE HILL – BLOODY BUSH – BOGGY BOTTOM – BROKENWIND – BROWN WILLY – BUSH GAP – BELL END.

Looking around the world it gets worse.

ARSOLI, ITALY – BALD KNOB, ARKANSAS – BENDERS LANDING, TEXAS – BIG BEAVER, SASKATCHEWAN – BIG BOGUE HOMO CREEK, MISSISSIPPI – BOBBIN HEAD, AUSTRALIA.

And you will notice that I haven't even got past the 'B's ...

So, sad as it may sound, each crossroads was looked forward to with great anticipation in the hope that I might see another ridiculously sounding village name.

Of course, the family do take up some thinking time too. Is my wife out, spending money on clothes she doesn't need? Are the kids still managing to stay out of prison? You know the routine – standard domestic stuff.

The final two things I think about are mind games and both mathematical. The first was a simple one. Every 10 miles I would have an energy drink or water, together with a Jaffa bar or piece of Kendal Mint Cake – eating on the hoof so to speak. Checking my odometer became an obsession but it kept me focussed. It was like saying: 'In one mile you can have a drink, so get a move on.'

The other one was slightly more complex. Within hours of leaving Land's End I was an expert on percentages. Again using my odometer I would regularly check how far I had travelled, how far I had to go, and guestimate my time of arrival. It was of paramount importance to me mentally to have completed at least 60 per cent of the day's ride before 1 p.m. If not, the afternoon became a terrible slog. All in the head you understand, but it gave me targets to go for and kept my mind active.

Ah, there was one other thought in my mind but so far it had not really been used, except possibly when I had crashed.

However, it would be though, when I was travelling through Scotland later in the ride.

The thought?

Survival.

Back on the road I was making good progress, crossing the Manchester Ship Canal as I weaved a course between Manchester and Liverpool. Just prior to taking an iron bridge over the canal I rode close to Lymm, a small town I remember from my days with Derby County – Reserves that is.

We always stopped for lunch at the grand hotel there before moving on for our annual hammerings in Manchester, Liverpool, Blackpool Blackburn, Bolton and Preston. It wasn't always bad news though – we usually murdered Bury.

We once got terribly excited after hearing that the great Brazilian team, including Pele, were staying in the same Lymm hotel during the 1966 World Cup. Our coach didn't share our emotions, merely muttering: 'It's a bloody pity a bit of their skill doesn't rub off on you lot.'

With little sign of hills I was making great progress in the warm sunshine, the day's ride turning out to be far smoother than I had anticipated. It was late morning and I hadn't got lost once.

I pressed on over the A580 and entered Wigan Borough, or more specifically, Leigh. It wasn't my first visit to the town having been there many times before to visit the Lunn Poly shop that was based there. One of our more successful travel shops, if my memory serves me correctly.

Leigh. A town of fast food shops that caters for every country, class and creed. In metaphorical terms, fast food was coming out of Leigh's ears. Travelling in on the A574, I couldn't move for outlets selling 'scran'. I am not lying when I tell you that I counted 8 shops in a row, all purveying food of a high calorific value that would have shot off the Richter scale were it to be used for that purpose. Thinking again, if a few of the people I saw outside the food stores had slipped and fell, the Richter scale would have come in very handy.

There were pizzas, chilli, chips, Indian, Tex Mex, pies, Chinese, Kebabs and Thai. There may have been more but my stomach rumbled so much it made my eyes water and restricted my view. Eventually the food shops gave way to tanning shops and bookies before they made up ground again with a burger bar and a fried chicken outlet.

Along with nail and beauty shops there was not much else other than pubs. With greengrocers selling fruit and vegetables conspicuous by their absence, it did cross my mind that Leigh, and Hanham in Bristol, would make good twinning towns.

'Never mind travelling to France or Germany for cordial relations me duck, lets all decamp down to Asda in the South-West for a blow out'.

My route took me right through the centre of town, a challenge for me during a busy lunchtime period. The cleats on my cycling shoes came in and out of the pedals more times, and quicker, than a fiddler's elbow playing an Irish jig as I was forced to slow down or stop for slow moving cars, buses and pedestrians.

As I crawled north out of town towards West Houghton I noticed a woman of irregular shape boarding a bus that was bound for Atherton, some three miles away. With the traffic moving slowly I was able to keep pace with the flow. Two minutes later I saw the woman again, this time waddling up the street. Now, I am not one to make assumptions, but I narrowed her motives for disembarking from the bus at the very next stop down to two options: on this hot and sunny day in early June my outsize lady did not have the energy to walk less than 200 yards between stops or, she had suddenly spotted a long lost fruit shop and was gagging for an apple. Go on, you guess first.

On I plodded, out of West Houghton up the busy A6 for the 10 miles to Chorley. It wasn't long before I caught a glimpse of the Reebok Stadium, the home of Bolton Wanderers. Quite naturally, as with the Alexandra Stadium in Crewe, a regulation stop was made and photographs duly taken for record purposes.

It was after one o'clock when I eventually pulled into Chorley, but before dropping down the slope into the centre of the town I stopped at the Spinners Arms for some liquid refreshment. I seemed to have been riding forever although it was actually less than five hours – the built-up areas of the North-West taking their toll on my concentration and energy.

I sat out on the wooden decking overlooking the town, quietly pleased with myself for having taken on many of the industrials towns of Greater Manchester and coming out on top. A pint of lager and a plate of tuna sandwiches I deemed a suitable reward.

Soon nine lads and their boss joined me for what I assumed was a brief lunchtime pint followed by a trip to Old Trafford for a Lancashire limited-overs cricket match. The usual banter ensued and it was easy to spot who the clowns were in the group and who the quiet ones were. One in particular was the centre of attention and was clearly enjoying the adoration of his mates. Whether they told him he was a born comedian or not I hesitate to judge, but my guess is that his Mum's biased view was an influence on his misplaced confidence.

Beer, sun, banter and sports chat. As I sat there observing, it all seemed to add up. Definitely a beer, then some cricket.

But, how wrong could I be?

Talking with the boss it turned out that cricket was not on the agenda at all – something far more serious had occurred.

The day before, the staff had arrived for work to find their office a burned out shell. The company sold advertising space, and all their records, along with business contracts, had gone up in smoke, completely destroyed by a fire. He would need to start again, but initially take a loss he estimated to be in the region of £50,000, on the chin. What amazed me was that they were all having a laugh and sharing jokes, including the boss.

While I can understand the merriment of the staff sitting in the sun drinking at the boss's expense, he too seemed to be very philosophical about the whole disaster.

What a man. I do hope he is back on his feet and, today, still laughing, along with his staff.

Chorley to Bashall Eaves, my overnight stop, was only 25 miles following the route laid down by the Cycling Touring Club, but somehow I managed to make it close to 35 miles.

It all looked so easy, weaving up the variety of B roads through Wheelton, Brindle, Hoghton, Mellor, Whalley and Great Mitton, but I made a right 'pig's ear' of it, managing to turn the instructions into an uphill slalom course.

Side to side I went like a yacht tacking against the wind, first west, then east, then west again, so it went on. It was a nightmare only broken by a snatched glance at Hoghton Tower and a mental reminder to investigate the stately home's history if I ever got out of the zigzag course I was on.

Hoghton Tower is a place I had never heard of until passing it, but it does have quite a history. Built in 1565 by Thomas Hoghton it has proved to be a versatile stately pile throughout the ages. William lll, George IV, Queen Mary and even Prince Philip have all popped in for coffee, as have William Shakespeare and Charles Dickens. I should add, not all at the same time.

However, of Hoghton's quest to be a social climber, the best story I could find was when King James attended a banquet there. In his honour a half-mile length of red carpet was laid from the gatehouse to the main house. It is not recorded whether the roll was returned to Allied Carpets the next day and/or whether a refund was given. I personally would have only given Mr Hoghton credit vouchers.

In latter days the grounds and house were used as film sets for *Moll Flanders*, starring Diana Rigg, as well as the TV series *Casanova*, with

David Tennant, prior to him finding fame with *Dr Who*.

Besides the inevitable picturesque gardens the house was available for all types of special occasions: weddings, anniversaries, funerals and Bar mitzvahs etc. etc. It also has the statutory gift shop.

But best of all, Hoghton Towers boasts an attraction that just about every detached house with more than six bedrooms boasts – it has a ghost and lays on regulation ghost tours at the dead of night.

My bet is that the ghost is Thomas Hoghton, pacing the house's corridors trying to work out where best to lay half a mile of Allied Carpet's best.

Eventually I chanced upon Walton-le-Dale and took my bearings. By taking the B6230 I could cut diagonally north-east, past the BAE Systems establishment at Samlesbury, then head up the A59 to Whalley and the minor B road to Bashall Eaves.

I was back on track even though the estimated distance of 76 miles at an average speed of a miserable 11.8 miles an hour was nothing I would ever be able to divulge to proper cyclists – or write home about for that matter.

It was about this time that I did meet a proper cyclist, or more to the point, he met me – by sneaking up from behind. We engaged in casual conversation as I deftly tried to raise my mundane speed by a mile or two an hour. This meant my new friend would have to do most of the talking, as any air that I was inhaling was devoted to keeping my bike moving forward – I had very little for talking except for the occasional: 'Well done you'.

Not only was he a keen cyclist, he was also a fell runner having competed in a 40 mile race over the Bowland Fells the previous weekend. He was as fit as a butcher's dog and also extremely polite, graciously congratulating me on my journey to-date – not that he had a clue about the route that I had taken due to me being unable to talk.

It was quite a blessing when he told me he was turning off to Ribchester, for if he had stayed with me much further it would have been necessary to summon the Red Cross and St John's Ambulance as I was way above my class. I do hope he caught the 'good luck' I gasped as he accelerated away.

Returning to my heavily fatigued crawl, I feared that the last 10 miles would feel like 20 and I was dead right, the minor road from Whalley up to Bashall Eaves seemingly going on for ever.

Eventually at 5.30 p.m. I reached Chapel Cottage at the base of the Bowland Fells and a warm welcome from my landlady for the night, Carole Baldwin.

My double room (at single rate) was superb, and, after a shower and change, I strolled the few hundred yards through the village to probably the best restaurant I ate in throughout my whole adventure, The Red Pump Inn.

It was early evening and the view from the pub/restaurant across to Kemple End, bathed in the slowly dipping sun, was simply staggering. There I was, the novice cyclist, who had just pedalled past everything that the north-west of England had to offer, now in open country and ready to attack the beautiful Forest of Bowland.

But that was for another day, first a couple of pints of Black Sheep had to be sunk along with some paté, braised beef and the inevitable sticky toffee pudding.

The establishment, run by a couple from Liverpool, was buzzing, it was clearly a popular hostelry that had earned a wonderful reputation and quite rightly so.

But there was just one flaw. When my bill arrived, the landlord had missed a pint from my account. Can you believe the incompetence of the man – probably the first Scouser in history to miss a trick.

I felt it would have been rude to draw the error to his attention and knock his confidence so I quickly paid up and strolled back to Chapel Cottage.

I was asleep by 9.45 p.m.

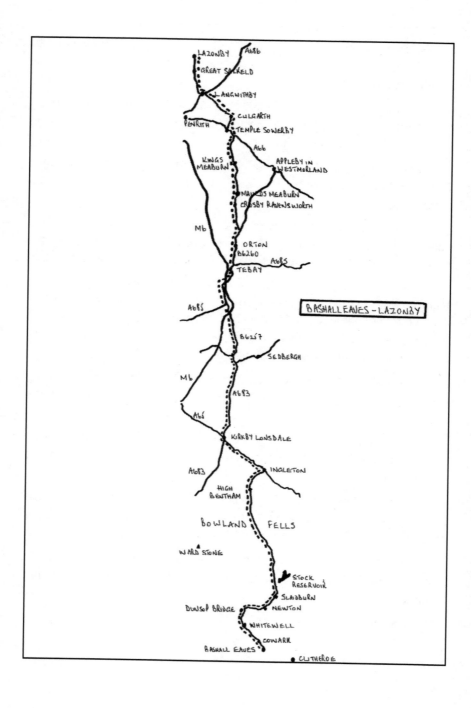

LAZONBY A686
GREAT SALKELD
LANGWITHBY
CULGARTH
PENRITH
TEMPLE SOWERBY
A66
KINGS
MEABURN
APPLEBY IN
WESTMORLAND
MAULDS MEABURN
CROSBY RAVENSWORTH
M6
ORTON
B6260
A685
TEBAY
A685
B6257
SEDBERGH
M6
A683
A66
KIRKBY LONSDALE
A683
INGLETON
HIGH
BENTHAM
BOWLAND FELLS
WARD STONE
STOCK
RESERVOIR
SLAIDBURN
DUNSOP BRIDGE
NEWTON
WHITEWELL
COWARK
BASHALL EAVES
CLITHEROE

BASHALL EAVES - LAZONBY

Overlooking St Michael's Mount and Penzance from Marazion.

Climbing out of Cheddar Gorge.

With son Thomas crossing the Severn Bridge.

Enthralled by raconteur Jack Leahy.

"Smelling the roses" at Ironbridge, Shropshire.

Route planning with Alan Durban and Ritchie Barker.

Climbing the Bowland Fells with John and Frances Barr.

The solitude and beauty of the Fells.

"Give me a sign". Crossing the border.

The Kagyu Samye Ling Tibetan Buddhist Centre in Eskdalemuir.

A wet Sunday on the Forth Road Bridge.

Looking back down Glenshee.

Not too far now as the Cromarty Forth comes into view.

Crossing the loch into Bonar Bridge.

Relaxing at the Falls of Loch Shin.

The lonely Crask Inn in Sutherland.

A busy "A" road overlooking Loch Naver near Altnaharra.

All that remains of the Highland Clearance at Grumbeg.

A busy "A" road overlooking Loch Naver near Altnaharra.

All that remains of the Highland Clearance at Grumbeg.

"Touch down" at John O'Groats.

"Well done you," said Prime Minister, David Cameron.

Day 8
Bashall Eaves to Lazonby

TODAY was to be a special day when I wouldn't be short of company. I was to be accompanied by a former business colleague, Colin Wilson and his friend Mark, each of them riding alternate 10 mile legs while the other followed by car.

The benefits to me were twofold – company across the quiet fells and a day when I could reduce some weight by unloading my panniers into the escort car.

With the weather again superb is was a pleasure to greet them outside my B&B although it did give me some concern to see Colin roll up in a green polo shirt, khaki pedal pusher shorts and sandals. He looked more like he was popping down to the newsagent's for a paper than going on a long distance ride. I half expected Postman Pat to drive by.

Colin and Mark spending a day with me was a long way away from the initial idea agreed several months earlier when I was planning the trip. Then, Colin and another business friend Gary Rook had intimated to me that they would be not only too happy to donate to my chosen charity, but also to join me on the ride.

That idea was then watered down – considerably. A late email told me that they would join me for only a day of my ride, and eventually another message confirmed that they would share a day of my ride with each of them alternating between bike and car. By any standards it was a considerably reduced commitment, but still a welcome gesture none the less.

Whatever, both lads are great company and it would be a pleasure to see them again and recall the fantastic times we had together while building the Lunn Poly chain of holiday shops.

Sadly, at the last minute Gary had to cry off for business reasons hence the arrival of Mark as his substitute – no bad thing as Mark was a keen photographer and I could look forward to some stunning shots of the fells.

However, I would miss Rooky's company as, to put it mildly, he was a bit of a character.

Let me give you an example.

Before I do though, let me introduce you to another 'character' – Mad Frankie Fraser.

Frankie Fraser was infamous in the 1960s, turning down an invite to join the Kray twins' gang preferring to team up with the Krays' bitter rivals Charlie and Eddie Richardson and their 'alleged' torture gang.

Frankie had all the credentials necessary to be a big timer for either side, his eventual career CV citing 28 convictions, 20 different prisons and 42 years behind bars. As one underworld colleague jested when he united with the Richardson gang: 'It was like China being given the Atom bomb'. Let's just leave it that Frankie could look after himself.

So, where does Rooky come into all this?

Well, Mr Fraser had spent a fair number of his years serving his time at Her Majesty's pleasure in Lincoln Jail, the city where Rooky lived and he thought it would be a good idea to invite Frankie to his home for the weekend as his guest. Rooky's thinking was that it was a marvellous opportunity to re-introduce him to his spiritual home.

God only knows how he got it past Sue his wife, but he did. I should add that by this time Frankie was well into his 70s, but as the saying goes, once a crook always a crook.

I think it is fair to say that if two Home Secretaries have described you as the most dangerous man in Britain you still pack a bit of a punch, whatever your age.

As an aside, if you happen to have Frankie Fraser's autobiography to hand take a look at the photograph of Frankie standing outside Lincoln Jail with 'some friends'. You'll see Rooky standing there with him – he's the one with the stupid smile.

Anyway, Frankie duly arrived at Lincoln railway station and Rooky collected him and took him straight to his local pub, 'The Strugglers', for a beer and an introduction to his mates.

Picture the scene. Frankie, possibly no more than 5' 4", 70-something, wearing a black heavy overcoat, white silk scarf and homburg hat, sitting in the Strugglers' snug, behind a glass of milk stout.

In came Dickie, a mate of Rooky's and, seeing mad Frankie, blurted out: 'Who the fuck has brought their grandad in here then?'

Total silence, in fact more than total silence. Frankie just sat there looking straight ahead while supping the froth from his drink. Make no mistake, he had heard the comment – everyone had heard the comment.

Rooky ushered Dickie away and quietly and sensitively explained who his guest was, plus a little bit about his background.

Exit Dickie from the Strugglers.

'Dickie not stopping for a drink then?' said the landlord.

Not stopping? Dickie was not only 'too busy' to stop for a drink, he didn't step into the Strugglers for a drink for fully two weeks. And only then after Rooky had sworn on his life that Frankie was back in the East End of London.

I thought of Frankie Fraser only a few months ago when reading an article in the press. Evidently his grandson, Tommy, played football for Barnet after being released by Port Vale. Legend has it that a local reporter from the *Barnet and Potters Bar Times* asked Tommy if his grandad ever watched him play. He was told: 'No, because he was very unhappy you only gave me 6 out of 10 in the game against Chesterfield'.

From that day on, Tommy never received less than an eight. Personally I'd have given him 11.

With stories like that you can understand why I was disappointed that Rooky couldn't make it, but I was more than happy to have Colin and Mark alongside me. The weather was perfect again and the scenery promising to be the best so far.

Colin took the first leg and, typical of his nature, before we had reached Cow Ark (another great name) was soon 100 yards ahead of me, his pedals going twice the speed of Mark Cavendish's in one of his sprint finishes. True to form, it was the classic tortoise and hare story unfolding, for within a mile the roles were reversed, the peloton of one – me – going past the early pacesetter.

The scenery was already beginning to change as we took the lane towards Whitewell before turning right and heading along the fells to Newton and Slaidburn.

How does one try to explain beautiful, raw and wild countryside, because mere words don't even begin to do justice to the views that were around us.

Shut your eyes and picture a sunny June morning, cloudless skies, a lane no more than 10 ft wide wending its way across fells that climb high to right and left. Below them were perfectly manicured, stone wall lined lush green fields housing gambolling lambs and their mothers. Add the odd stone isolated building and a profusion of colour from the early summer wild flowers and you might just come close to visualising the scene.

They say that a picture paints a thousand words – how true.

Beauty or no beauty, the going was tough, the gradual but challenging climbs seemingly going on forever until the joy of reaching the top and free wheeling down the other side.

It was my first time in the Forest of Bowland and I rapidly learned it is not a Forest at all – the word in the true sense meaning a Royal hunting ground. It's also known as the Trough of Bowland although Bowland Fells is a much more accurate description. Designated an area of natural beauty as late as 1964, it is not described as the Switzerland of England for nothing.

Surprisingly the Forest of Bowland area is not often visited by tourists – most of them prefer to hare up the M6 motorway and on to the Lake District. Take my word for it though, the wild beauty and deserted roads are perfect for cyclists, walkers, photographers, even fell runners, plus anyone else who wants to clear their heads from urban noise and pressure. If you are visiting the Lake District, spare a day for the Bowland Fells – you will not be disappointed.

In the Fells there are 11 hills over 1,000 ft high – the highest being Ward's Stone at 1,841ft, over 500 listed buildings and 18 monuments. To add to these geographical accolades, just north of Dunlop Bridge is the absolute centre of Great Britain.

For me it was turning into an unforgettable day, and, with a friend old and new, it was more like the Centre of the Universe than the Centre of Great Britain.

To paraphrase Arnold Schwarzenegger from the science fiction film, *The Terminator*: 'I'll be back'.

Within the hour we were in Slaidburn, stopping for a photo call outside the 'Hark and Bounty' inn. Already there, were a couple from Edinburgh who were just returning from a cycling trip to the Pyrenees.

John and Frances Barr were both in the early sixties and had been cycling together for over 30 years. Not for them the luxury of bed and breakfasts, this couple were hardy campers as could be seen by the two enormous packs on each of their bikes. John's was particularly awesome, the size and weight of his panniers more likely to be spotted on the back of a Peruvian pack horse.

They had left home on 20 April and had cycled through England and France to Perpignan, and were returning home to plan their next adventure

– riding round the total coastline of Australia.

My 'End-to-End' journey of 1,100 miles sounded so insignificant compared to the feats of these four wheeled knights of the road, and I felt humble as we joined forces to continue our ride over the fells.

I felt guilty riding without panniers, especially as John's load looked to be well in excess of 50 lb, and, after gushing apologies about the unfairness of the situation, together we attacked the even steeper climbs up and over the stark Croasdale and Tatham Fells close by Stock reservoir and Gisburn Forest before stopping in High Bentham for coffee.

The section with John and Frances was only 12 miles, but what a wonderful 12 miles it was. Fantastic scenery, even better than earlier in the day, plus enthralling stories told by possibly the most modest man ever to mount a bike. It was like pulling teeth to extract from him the fact that he had undergone a hip replacement only a year earlier and had pins inserted in his shoulder following a cycling accident. They certainly breed them tough at Musselburgh Cycling Club.

We talked about our journeys and I mentioned Guy and Jason, the two lads I had shared my first night with way back in the Ship Inn in Wadebridge a week earlier. John told me that Jason was still battling his way north having stopped for a chat with himself and Frances when overtaking them in Leigh a day or two earlier – a coincidence that, to me, made the world just that little bit smaller.

Many months later when giving a talk on my ride to the Round Table in Derby I mentioned my brief time with John and Frances, and afterwards one of the members came up to me and told me that he had enjoyed a very nice chat with them on the Portsmouth to Santander ferry only a few weeks earlier. Where will they turn up next?

Leaving the Barrs at High Bentham we made good progress along the fast but undulating A65 through Ingleton and Kirkby Lonsdale, then turned right on to the A683 that headed north in the direction of Sedbergh. It was here that I had my first puncture after well over 500 miles of riding.

One of the things I had learned from my training rides was to be extra careful when riding under trees when the sun is shining. The light and shade of the sun's rays through the leafy branches leave a dappled effect on the road and make potholes much more difficult to spot. On this occasion I was a victim, the weight over my back wheel making the tyre succumb to the sudden pressure when I hit the edge of the hole.

Sod's law meant that all my repair equipment was in my panniers in the back up car, and the back up car was nowhere to be seen. Easy I thought, Colin can call Mark on his mobile, tell him where we are and in no time at all we will be off and running.

Sadly no. Colin did not have Mark's mobile number so Plan 'B' had to come into play.

Suffice to say, tracking down Mark's number was not easy. First it entailed calling Colin's wife in Stratford-upon-Avon, her running round to Mark's house to get his mobile number then ringing us back so we could make a call. Good for Vodafone's revenue no question, but not too good for my patience.

Even when we got through to Mark it wasn't easy explaining exactly where we were, me quickly realising that telling him we were in a quiet lane with trees over the top was insufficient for him to home in on us. As you can imagine it took some time for him to arrive and a new inner tube to be fitted. Not so much a backup car, more a cock-up car.

It took 90 minutes from puncturing to getting back on the road – in between times I had to endure the dry and sardonic wit of my great friend Anton Rippon who was sitting cosily in the Masons Arms in Mickleover, Derby imbibing with his mates. I should have withstood the jibes that came down the telephone line and turned the other cheek, but, to be fair, we were still less than halfway to Lazonby, our night stop, and it was already 2.45 p.m.

Whether Anton was able to put his pint of beer where I suggested is not known, but just saying it made me feel a tad better.

Temporarily dejected by the delay and bemoaning that I had left the basic repair equipment out of my sight we pressed on, Mark now taking over from Colin as my co-rider. Regardless of who it was accompanying me my complete focus was on getting to Lazonby as speedily as possible, with or without them.

The scenery was still stunning as we moved from the A683 just outside Sedbergh on to the B6257 heading for Tebay, our ride only spoiled by the constant criss-crossing of the noisy M6 motorway. One minute we were 300 ft above it, the next 200 ft below. A pain, but the viaducts did provide a good backdrop for photographs.

Tebay eventually came into view at 5 p.m. and it was beginning to look like an 8 p.m. finish – if we were lucky. The countryside was now a lot flatter – we were off the fells and on to more orthodox farmland with tiny hamlets dotted every few miles. The sight of a very attractive cricket ground confirmed that we were back into civilisation.

With over eight hours on and off the road under our belts we were pretty exhausted. However, Lady Luck had already joined us – gone were the desperately hard climbs we had endured for most of the day in temperatures above 70 degrees, making way for roads with steady undulations, interspersed with occasional short climbs and descents.

After first taking the B6260 to Orton we turned on to a lane, knowing that Lazonby could not be too far away. In my mind neither was a pint. Through Crosby Ravensworth and Mauld Meaburn we raced followed by Kings Meaburn, Temple Sowerby and Culgaith, its quaint railway crossing over the road providing another photo opportunity for Mark.

A quick look at the map told us that when we had crossed the A686 main road from Penrith to Newcastle-upon-Tyne and ridden through Langwathby and Great Salkeld we would be very close to our goal.

At last, at 7.15 p.m with the day still bright with sunshine I saw the wonderful sign of Lazonby welcoming us. Another day was under my belt.

Almost 10 hours on the road, a miserly 76 miles, but there were extenuating circumstances – mountainous fells and a puncture to name just two.

There was just time to say hello to Eileen O'Neil my Lazonby landlady and, at her request, hand over my dirty washing, before retiring to the Midland Hotel for a couple of swift pints with Colin and Mark. It would have been more but they were both committed to pushing on by car to Penrith for dinner with Colin's sister. Only halfway down his first pint he swore he could smell her rabbit stew on the hob.

All too soon they were gone.

After the long, hot and extremely fruitful day I decided to stay put at the Midland Hotel. I ordered a third pint of beer along with spaghetti bolognaise and my ever faithful sticky toffee pudding and reflected on what great value for money I was getting for under a tenner.

I can heartily recommend the Midland Hotel in Lazonby – it's a good old-fashioned, no-frills pub that sells good food and great ale at affordable prices. But there are a few words of caution. Refrain from trying to get into conversation with the landlord – he doesn't do words. Put it this way, he looked like Herman Munster and was more miserable than a funeral director at his own cremation. I would be willing to bet that there will be a total eclipse of the sun before he laughs, and I know for a fact that the next eclipse is not until 2079.

Friday night in the Midland was a good place to be, with or without a genial host, and tomorrow I would be in Scotland.

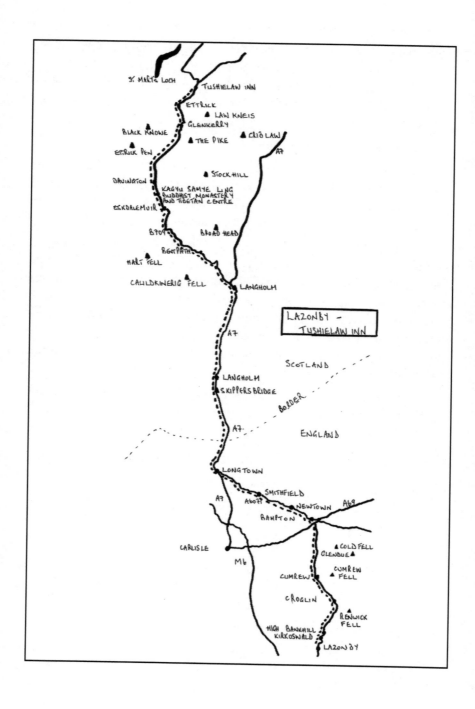

Day 9
Lazonby to Tushielaw

I HAD been on the road for 8 days now and with few exceptions had come through my ride unscathed. I knew it would be tough, I knew it would be lonely, even accepting the fact that I had enjoyed two days with some company.

But now my friends and family were behind me and the road ahead, across the border and right through Scotland, was still to be ridden – alone.

I was also was under no illusions that there were still many challenges ahead. Yes, the first two days through Cornwall and Devon had been early tests but the following five, with a few exceptions, had been relatively smooth, give or take the odd lumpy bit or two.

Yesterday had had its share of steep pulls but the weather had been beautiful, we had travelled slowly, and I had been pannier-free. Today I was on my own and the panniers were back. Would they make much of a difference?

I didn't think for one second that Scotland would let me ride through it and leave without reminding me that, while its hinterland may be beautifully rugged and an enticement for motorised tourists, it positively ate up two-wheeled travellers.

It would be a battle between the terrain and me.

My first target was easy to define. By midday I wanted to be over the border and boast that I had 'ridden' England. Then I could concentrate on Scotland.

Unbelievably, another warm, sunny morning greeted me as I left Lazonby at 9.15 a.m. to travel up to the Tushielaw Inn deep in the Ettrick Valley.

Within 20 minutes of leaving Lazonby I was brought back to the harsh realities of life: riding with panniers again. The extra 24 lb compared to yesterday, gave me the impression I was riding with my back brake on, such was the 'drag', and already I was kicking myself for taking the easy way out over the Bowland Fells the day before.

The inclines through the first two villages of Kirkoswald and High Bankhill were far and away the worst I had encountered since Devon, and, with tiredness still in my legs from the exertions in the fells, there was only one thing for it: I walked.

Based on my experience of the first two villages I came to, I even changed out of my cycling shoes with cleats and into my trainers. How about that for my confidence levels? Of course, sod's law being what it is, after High Bankhill I didn't walk for the rest of the day.

Out of High Bankhill I took the lane towards Cumrew and hit some first-rate cycling roads – I simply bowled along, past neatly cultivated fields with sheep grazing, while high to my right was the continuing backdrop of Renwick and Cumrew Fells. The good news was, that even with my limited map reading abilities, the last few Fells of the Bowlands would not be troubling me today.

In the first 75 minutes of riding I had covered a very satisfying 16 miles, already nearly 25 per cent of the 68 that I had set myself for the day. Nice start I thought, at this rate I would be at the Tushielaw Inn by 3.00 p.m., 3.30 p.m. at the latest if I stopped somewhere for a coffee and cake.

After Cumrew the countryside slowly changed from manicured fields to wilder, craggier slopes and grazing sheep. Desolate reddish-brown stone Cumbrian farmhouses occasionally broke the barren landscape, but even in the June sun it was easy to imagine just how tough pasture farming would be in the winter months on the slopes of Glendue and Cold Fells.

My mind wandered back to my Lazonby B&B and the breakfast table I had shared with a couple from Bristol. They told me they had ridden over from the Lake District and had excellent reasons for doing so.

Two days earlier, police, giving no explanation, had diverted the train they had been travelling on near Workington into a siding. Soon they would learn why, together with the whole of the country.

It was the day of the mass murders in Cumbria when 12 innocent people lost their lives at the hands of Derrick Bird. A lone cyclist had been one of his victims. Amazingly, the couple seemed in good spirits even though, unbeknown to them at the time, they had been within a few miles of a madman with a gun.

As I continued towards the border it was around this time too that I began to think of the Roman Emperor Hadrian and a piece of building work that he had commissioned back in 122 AD. My head gave a very realistic impression of a ventriloquist's dummy as my eyes roamed the landscape for the broken line of stone I was seeking. There were hundreds of stone walls visible, but alas none that told me I had found Hadrian's Wall, or any Romans come to that.

A northerly headwind had sprung up just before I passed through Brampton that made life a little uncomfortable for me, but it soon changed to a cross wind when I turned on to the A6071 to head more westerly through Newtown and Smithfield to Longtown. I made Longtown my next target, with the promise of a coffee and cake if I had averaged at least 12 miles an hour following my departure from Lazonby.

I also promised myself I would write a stiff letter to the Cumbria County Council suggesting to them that they may like to get off their fat backsides in their comfortable offices in Carlisle and take a good long look at the state of the A6071 road surface.

If they had already looked and seen no cause for action my next piece of advice to them would have been to visit Specsavers.

For an A road the surface was dire, nay a death trap for cyclists, with potholes more numerous than sand grains in the Sahara. It was a case of death by pothole or HGV as I slalomed towards my coffee break.

The Gretna Bakery and Café was my host at Longtown and the coffee and large meringue priced at £3.50 most welcome. I was now only three miles south of the Scottish border but was intrigued by the accents of the locals. They were all speaking with a Scottish brogue. For Christ's sake why? They were English and living in an English town.

People in Dover don't speak French, Welsh isn't the native tongue in Chester – get a bloody grip I thought as I listened to the shoppers jabbering away. You're still in dear old Blighty – stand tall and proud.

Making a mental note to check whether the 'Jocks' spoke with an English accent three miles north of the border, I pressed on and reached 'Check Point Sporran' at exactly five minutes after noon.

Scotland was welcoming me. In fact, Scotland was welcoming me many times.

The first sign, a blue one with a patriotic white cross, told me I was: 'Welcome to Scotland' as well as 'Failte gu Alba' which I took to be an anagram. To this day I am still wrestling with that unsolved word game.

Forty yards distant was another sign, the local council getting in on the act with a 'Welcome to Dumfries and Galloway'. Underneath, in smaller lettering was: 'First in Scotland' which I took to be pretty obvious unless some small 'Duchy' had suddenly mushroomed in the gap between the two signs.

Then a further 20 yards on was a normal road sign explaining that I was on the A7 and that Hawick and Galashiels were waiting to welcome me to their bosoms.

Finally after another 25 yards, a digital sign telling me that there were traffic delays ahead. You couldn't make it up.

Just to be on the safe side I checked my map, and, sure enough, it confirmed that I had left England. My CTC route finder also corroborated that fact. I was indeed abroad.

So I rode on, confident that John O'Groats was somewhere up in front.

From Longtown I stayed on the A7 for the nine mile stretch to Langholm. It wasn't particularly busy being a Saturday – lorry drivers having a day off and football fans non-existent, except at Parkhead and Ibrox.

A couple of miles before I reached Langholm I stopped to take a photograph of my first Scottish river flowing under a stone bridge.

Little did I know I would see 33,711 more before I reached my destination. But I will always have a soft spot for the River Esk at Skippers Bridge, for it was my first.

Interestingly for older readers, my research unearthed the fact the James Robertson Justice, a popular actor in the 'Doctor' comedy films of the 50s and 60s was born in Langholm. Evidently his mother was passing through the town on her way to Edinburgh while in the later stages of her pregnancy, and out popped JRJ. Bet she needed forceps.

At Langholm, I left the A9, turning north-east on to the B709 and my first real taste of raw, unspoiled Scottish countryside. I was closing in on Eskdalemuir 10 miles away and mid distance to the Tushielaw Inn, where I was staying overnight.

I was now on what must be the quietest B road in Great Britain, and, in the 50 minutes or so it took me to climb to Eskdalemuir, I can honestly say that I did not see one vehicle.

No cars but plenty of sheep, millions of them, maybe more. And that is not including the lambs that stood by the roadside before scuttling back to their mothers when I encroached within a few yards of them. It confirmed to me that even lambs are brainless. They could see me coming from 100 yards away but left it until the last second before running away. Better anticipation (or eyesight) would have led to a leisurely stroll back to mum instead of having to complete a Usain Bolt type sprint.

I also took umbrage at the way they looked at me, possibly one sure sign how the heat of the day was affecting me. They were giving me the impression that I was stupid and had no right to interrupt or gate crash them as they jumped and twitched in a weird compulsorily epileptic manner along the roadside verges of their vast playground.

I suppose, with me fast approaching old age, wearing colourful Lycra and riding a bike 1,100ft up Cauldkinerig Fell in the middle of nowhere, they had a reasonable point.

Little did they know that the lush green grass they were consuming was leading up to their very last supper and the final laugh would be with me – soon we would be meeting again – at my dinner table.

The road wound round high peaks, with Hart Fell to my left and Broad Head to my right, and, although it still required the occasional 'hard shift' on the pedals, it was a truly glorious place to be; sun shining, staggering scenery and total solitude – what more could a man ask for?

Besides sheep, the other major industry in the Borders is lumber and there were vast tracts of forest that had been ripped out by heavy machinery, replaced by small saplings – the timber of tomorrow. Or to be more precise, about 30 years' time.

It was sad to see so many ugly scars left on the land where huge areas of woodland had been cleared, but I dismissed my thinking as being naïve – nature and good lumber husbandry in the months and years ahead would soon heal this momentary blot on the landscape.

Eskdalemuir features strongly in the news whenever severe weather conditions are discussed. History tells us that in 1620, snow fell for 13 consecutive days, the depth so great and the temperatures so low that only 35 out of a flock of 20,000 sheep survived. That's an awful lot of dead carcasses.

Mischievously I couldn't help musing. Nowhere in the reference book that provided these figures does it state whether snow also fell for

13 consecutive nights. Nowhere does it state that the figure of 20,000 was an exact one and not an estimate and nowhere does it name the individual who counted the flock. Call me a stickler for accuracy but give me facts, not fiction, every time.

The name of the sheep counter may well have been a long lost relation of Donald McTavish, the former Scottish sheep-counting Champion. After winning the title for the seventh consecutive year, in an interview on TV, he was asked to explain how he was able to count sheep quicker than anyone else.

'Aye, it's a little secret, but I'll share it with you now I'm retiring. I count their legs and tails – then divide by five'.

Between Eskdalemuir and Davington I came across a vision that literally brought me to a standstill.

There I was, one minute serenely riding through the rolling border countryside, so familiar with the sheep that I was on nodding terms with many, even adding on at least two occasions my condolences for the 1620 snowfall. One ewe I spoke to was so old I would have bet a few bob that her grandmother had perished in the terrible blizzard. In short, I had been building a few relationships. I was a long way from home, lonely, and yes, I suppose I was grooming.

The next minute, as I reached the top of yet another lamb-clad hill, strolling towards me was a short, close-cropped, rimless spectacled person in long saffron robes, looking as if they had not a care in the world.

A perfect example of someone knee-deep in peace and tranquillity.

Not a perfect model for a hairdresser's in Knightsbridge I grant you, but a great advert for a local farmer looking to increase his share of the sheep shearing market.

Having never met a person meeting this description before I was unsure how to acknowledge them. You just don't know do you?

'Aye up youth' seemed too coarse, while a deep bow and a tug of the forelock a bit over the top. In my defence, I would defy anyone, except the best Buddhist in the world, to identify whether it was even a male or a female.

In the little thinking time I had available I eventually resorted to a hastily prepared smile with just the hint of a wink. That appeared to pass muster, as the smile was returned, although sadly no wink was forthcoming. Maybe if I rode past again?

I then rounded a corner, and in front of me was a building and grounds that would have been more at home in the foothills of the Himalayas. A full blown, no expense spared, in your face, Tibetan Monastery.

The structure had to be seen before it could be believed:

Strangely shaped, multicoloured ornate buildings with gold leaf roofs, fountains, an arched wooden bridge to an island in the centre of a small lake, manicured gardens with carvings and everywhere, bright flapping bunting waving in the breeze. The soft sound of wind chimes completed a truly astonishing sight.

Different I thought, definitely different.

The Kagyu Samye Ling Buddhist Monastery and Tibetan Centre, the first in the Western hemisphere, was built in 1967, and additional buildings were added over the Millennium period following the Dalai Lama giving the site his blessing in 1984.

Situated on the banks of the River Esk it is a centre of learning and wisdom, open to all faiths as well as those with none. In our parlance, I suppose it would be called a broad church.

Without wishing to be controversial, I saw it two ways. If your head needed clearing, this was the place to be and if it was already empty there was just a chance that it would have something in it before you left. The monastery was definitely a 'win-win' establishment.

From Kagyu Samye Ling monastery I rode on with an empty head and a less cynical mind, up the long incline to Glenkerry and Ettrick, the newly laid smooth road easing the friction on my tyres as I climbed steadily in the early afternoon sun.

Like so much of my cycling adventure to date I was becoming more and more frustrated with my inability to aptly describe the fantastically spectacular surroundings that I was passing through. Oh to be a John Betjeman or William Wordsworth.

'Green fertile lowlands, with sheep lazily grazing, thick forests neatly squared, patiently waiting the woodman's chainsaw. Soft babbling burns making their way over stony beds as they descended towards their collecting station, the proud River Esk. All under the watchful gaze of the magnificent high fells of Ettrick Pen, Crib Law, Black Knowe and Law Kneis.'

Truly the area could be called the proud border country.

No traffic, unforgettable scenery, perfect razor-sharp visibility, my bike and me. My own little world, shared with a few thousand innocent lambs. The memory will last long in my mind of that perfect Saturday in June.

Go there one early summer's day and embrace the scene. Tell the sheep I sent you – you won't be disappointed.

After leaving the small settlement of Ettrick I only had 3 miles to travel to the Tushielaw Inn, the home of Wendy and Robin Whitehead, my guardians for my first night in Scotland.

Looking back overall, I had eight nights north of the border and do you know what? Every single bed and breakfast and small hotel I stayed in was run by a foreigner – to Scotland that is.

Wendy was from Nuneaton, and later on in the week I would stay with a Mancunian, Londoner, Mexican, Yorkshireman and Geordie. Oh, and a gentleman who had spent all his life in the RAF, so I will call him unattached. Not a Scotsman in sight. They must have all migrated south to Corby or New Zealand – or maybe Canada.

I had an interesting welcome party when I walked into the Tushielaw

Inn at 4 p.m. The landlord was in bed following a rather heavy night, the landlady, God knows where, and the bar, which I was most interested in, overseen by two of their friends from Edinburgh.

I didn't cause a fuss; as far as I was concerned, after riding 68 miles from Lazonby, if Jack the Ripper or ET had pulled me a pint it would still have tasted the same.

The Tushielaw Inn is an old coaching inn, set in a tiny community in the triangle of famous border towns, Hawick, Moffat and Selkirk. It's an area renowned for walking and fishing holidays and has a wealth of wildlife – otters, hares, Roe deer, in addition to birds such as the oyster catcher, goosander and dipper.

And do know what? I never saw one, not even a stray cat. Just goes to show the power of marketing, eh?

About halfway down my first pint Wendy showed up and told me that there was one place to dine that evening: her place. After a nanosecond's thought I gratefully accepted her kind, albeit compulsory, invitation, before retiring to the bath, then the top of my bed to catch up on the latest offering the *Daily Mail* could bring to this neck of the woods.

I dined alone on my usual fayre of paté, pasta and sticky toffee pudding, and I was about to retire for the evening when Wendy informed me that there would be a ceilidh (pronounced Kaily) starting at 10.00 p.m. and that the bar was directly below my room. She also told me firmly that the late finish of the ceilidh would mean that I had no chance of my breakfast until at least eight o' clock the next morning.

I could not deduce whether her news was an apology, warning or invite so stared back at her, blowing out my cheeks and nodding.

As no alternative room was offered I took the information of the 'knees-up' to be more of a threat than a promise, so headed off to my quarters and the coffee time crossword of the Mail.

I was asleep with the fairies well before the first notes were struck at 10 that night and never heard a thing.

Leaving the Tushielaw Inn the next morning at a shade before nine I never did get the opportunity see l Robin, the landlord. I can only assume he had had another late night.

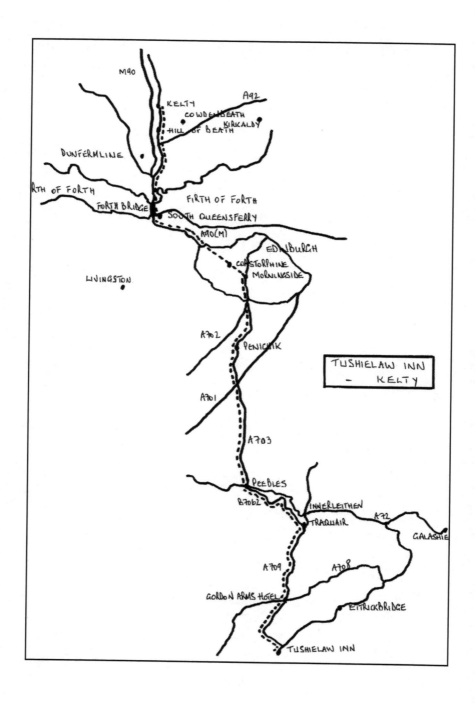

Day 10
Tushielaw to Kelty

MY biggest challenge of the day would be how to circumnavigate Edinburgh on my way, across the Firth of Forth, to Kelty a small village just north of Dunfermline in Fife.

I had been warned that the Edinburgh ring road was out of bounds to cyclists but numerous cycle paths were available, in fact so numerous and complex that it was highly likely that I could arrive back at my point of origin very easily.

Eventually I decided to take the sound advice and directions from Wendy's friend, Derek from Edinburgh, the first person I had met when arriving at the Tushielaw Inn the previous afternoon. He had suggested that I ignore the scenic lanes to the capital and, from Peebles, head straight up the A703 through Penecuik.

But all the advice in the world would have to wait a few hours as I still had the vast Ettrick Forest to plough through until I reached Traquair and a modicum of humanity.

On an overcast day I set off from Tushielaw with the dismal news that rain was forecast later in the day.

Rain? Major roads? Plotting my way through Edinburgh? Quite a challenge.

The memory of the Ross-on-Wye bypass soaking came flooding back, quite literally, although, with it being a Sunday, I was confident that many HGV drivers would be spending the Sabbath at rest.

Sadly the beautiful scenery I had encountered a day earlier had not been sustained and it was now long, long arduous diagonal climbs up the sides of steep fells. Even in the less than perfect visibility I could see that the road went on for miles with no discernible highlights. The view to my left was a long drop to the bottom of a valley and a burn that trickled slowly under a series of stone footbridges, while on my right, high ground reaching endlessly out of sight up into the low cloud. Put simply, it was just myself, out in the wilds, with my old trusty friends – sheep.

Now let me be clear here, I was not complaining, well not a lot. While the scenery was not as spectacular as yesterday's and was also marred by the cloud and mizzle in the air, it was still a million per cent better than riding through the suburbs of West Bromwich, Dudley or Walsall. No offence to my West Midlands readers but I really do mean that – much better. It was just that I had been spoiled by the stunning day previous and my mind was already becoming dulled by the fear of being lost in Edinburgh.

Anyone flying by helicopter and looking down would have seen a lone cyclist slowly pedalling at no more than 8 or 9 miles an hour up the long and straight B709 towards Traquair, with not another human within 15 miles – just a sheep population the size of Mumbai and Shanghai combined, to wish him well.

In fact, to relieve the boredom and tedium, I resorted to counting sheep as I rode by, quickly kicking that idea into touch when I found my eyes beginning to close as sleep approached.

Seasoned cyclists will understand me when I say that I relieved the monotony by fiddling with my gears. High and tired gears or low and slow? I forsook the extra 2 miles an hour speed and went for low and slow.

After what seemed like a lifetime, but was probably only about 90 minutes, I came off the pass and turned left into Traquair, a small place a couple of miles south of Innerleithen. A little lane cut the corner off the A709, giving me a short cut to Peebles that took me past Traquair House, a grand Scottish stately home built on the banks of the River Tweed.

The house's major claim to fame was proudly displayed on a sign at its entrance. It said boldly: 'Traquair House, the oldest continually inhabited house in Scotland.'

Now just wait a minute here, how do they know?

I can only conclude that they can support the claim in one of two ways. Option one, in 1107 they Googled the whole of Scotland for proof. Option two, and on a personal note I'm going with this one, the mistress of the house said,

'Campbell, before I put this sign up, put those bloody bagpipes down, get off your fat Scottish rump and have a stroll round the Glens to see if we have any neighbours shacking up within 30,420 square miles of this Caledonian hell-hole of ours.'

Editors note: For perfectionists, the figure stated above includes the mainland plus the 186 nearby islands, most of which can be found in the Hebrides, Orkneys and Shetlands.

Traquair House's other proud boast is that it has been visited by 27 Scottish Kings and Queens. Now, note the word Scottish in there. As you know, my strength isn't history but, to my knowledge, the last time Scotland had a King or a Queen was when human beings were running around dragging their knuckles on the ground.

Today, the house, is owned by the 21st Lady of Traquair (records don't say what happened to the other 20) and boasts beautiful gardens, a maze, craft workshops and a restaurant. Of particular interest to me was to learn that they even had their own micro-brewery. Things have certainly moved on since old Campbell went on tour.

I entered Peebles with the express wish to hunt down a pharmacy to seek advice for my badly gashed hip that had taken on a red and yellow colour besides oozing an interesting looking pus. Riding up and down its wide thoroughfare I located two, but both of them were closed.

How the good burghers of a town with 10,000 inhabitants and coach loads of geriatric tourists can allow both pharmacies in their town to remain closed on a busy Sunday is a complete and utter mystery to me. If I had been younger I would have seriously thought about plugging the gap in the market. Instead I decided that I didn't like Peebles, especially on Sundays.

I did manage to find a small coffee shop, however, and ventured to the first floor room for some much needed sustenance, a re-pack of my panniers and a look at the map for my next leg to Edinburgh. The map basically told me to get on to the A703 out of Peebles and ask again when I got to Edinburgh.

Just outside Peebles I took a call from my wife Christine and reassured her I was back in the land of the living after a morning on the moors. I also took the opportunity to don my rain jacket due to the morning drizzle having now changed to a steady downpour. In hindsight quite a good move as the damned rain persisted for the next six hours.

I imagined that Penicuik and Edinburgh were a greater distance from Peebles than they actually turned out to be, so my damp spirits were lifted when I saw that they were only 14 and 23 miles respectively further up the road. My spirits were further uplifted when the flat Scottish A703 allowed me to bowl along at an extremely tidy 18 miles an hour, heady stuff indeed after my morning fighting my way up from Tushielaw.

Just prior to Penicuik was a long, slow haul but I was ahead of schedule, so took the challenge manfully on the chin, grateful that I had travelled a dozen miles in miserable conditions in not much more than 45 minutes.

On the outskirts of the town I caught up with a very heavily laden 'End-to-Ender' who had left Land's End a good week before me. Strapped to his bike was a guitar. Its owner told me that he was busking his way up the line. I said nothing except: 'Well done, a brilliant idea'.

Immediately I thought back to 1966 when Allan Smethurst, a simple soul from Norfolk calling himself the 'Singing Postman', got into the charts with a catchy tune entitled 'Hev yew gotta loight boy'.

No, don't ask, he didn't have a follow up hit.

Sadly, Alan developed an alcohol problem and died in a Salvation Army hostel in Grimsby in December 2000.

Let's hope the cycling crooner has better luck.

I bade him farewell and pedalled on through Penicuik, the rain forming puddles on the road, making it difficult to identify the ruts and potholes conveniently placed for the unsuspecting cyclist. I occasionally looked back to see if the mobile busker was anywhere to be seen but he was gone, no doubt to sing a couple of songs that would pay for his lunch.

It was only another 40 minutes and the outskirts of Edinburgh came into sight. Following Derek's (from the Tushielaw Inn) advice I crossed over the busy ring road and moved from the A703 to the A702 to head north-west through Morningside towards the west end of Prince's Street.

I was feeling dejected from the steady rain that had been falling since Peebles ,but perked up slightly when I saw the Hilton Caledonian Hotel at the end of Princes Street, one of Britain's most attractive shopping boulevards.

I was now back on familiar territory, this part of the city being where I had opened some holiday shops in my former life, and I smartly turned due west and set my sights on Corstorphine and my first glimpse of the road signs for the Forth Bridge.

It was now moving towards late afternoon and all I had eaten since Tushielaw were my trusty Jaffa bars and Kendal Mint Cake, not a brilliant strategy, but one that would have to do until I was in the warmth of my Kelty B&B.

I only had about 10 miles to go to reach the Bridge and I felt a slight pang of excitement knowing that I would soon be crossing another famous landmark as I toiled north.

Soon I was at the A90, the major road that leads to South Queensferry and the crossing over the Firth of Forth. But a closer look at the A90 sign showed that my journey would end right there unless an enforced detour was made. It was clearly spelt out in blue and white on the road sign.

A90(M) NO PEDESTRIANS OR CYCLISTS.

Now, put yourself in my wet shoes. The Forth Road Bridge is almost in sight and the sign is saying that I cannot proceed. Would you or wouldn't you?

It didn't take long for me to come to an answer.

I reasoned that although the A90 was technically the A90 (M) thus making it a motorway, anyone riding in spectacles that had become blurred by heavy rain could quite easily miss the 'M' from the sign therefore making it the A90 again.

Off I went, rehearsing my reasoned excuse should I be pulled over by a patrolling police car. I even rehearsed a long apologetic diatribe finishing with the line that it was my first offence since leaving Cornwall and could I go on for just a teeny bit further.

Luck was with me and I stealthily cycled the 8 miles down the motorway to the Forth Bridge scared to death that every car coming up from behind was full of officers from the Midlothian police. When I reached my destination and looked across the grey waters to Fife I almost wet my pants with excitement – another famous landmark reached.

I hadn't realised that the Forth Bridge had only opened as recently as 1964, prior to that vehicles, cyclists and pedestrians were conveyed across the Forth by ferry. Ferry cross the Forth – hasn't quite got the same ring to it as Gerry Marsden's mega hit record involving the Mersey has it?

I read somewhere that the Bridge had some structural issues and with 60,000 cars going over at peak periods experts say that its 120-year life-span could be halved. Take my tip, make a note in your diary not to go anywhere near the place after 2024, it could be a death trap. All I was interested in was ensuring that it remained standing for a further 10 minutes so I could cross the one and a half-mile span.

But first a photograph was required for posterity.

I noted a lone walker heading towards me so asked him if he would be kind enough to take my photo. Standing with my bike, wearing my helmet, high-vis rain jacket and cycling shorts with the Forth Bridge as a backdrop would look pretty cool in my commemorative album.

It immediately became clear that I had made contact with a man who could not speak a word of English. He walked over to me jabbering away in some foreign tongue that may well have been Russian or Polish, possibly Albanian, or even Serbian. It definitely wasn't English, even with a Glaswegian accent.

I asked again if he would take a photo for me, this time pointing at the camera to give him a clue. Say what you like about me, but I do like to play fair with any foreign visitors to our shores.

He continued to rattle on at a fair rate of knots – all the correct letters of the alphabet, but in the wrong bloody order. While gabbling away in an animated state his hand shot into his inside jacket pocket and fumbled about for the object he was seeking.

Stroll on I thought; here am I, standing on the Forth Bridge, soaking wet, just wanting my picture taken and here is some foreign nutter, probably an illegal immigrant, going to shoot me. My initial thought was, if I am shot dead, how is my bike going to get home?

Fortunately, it wasn't a gun he pulled from his coat but a wad of ID papers. He thrust them towards me. Then the penny dropped. Johnny Foreigner had been thinking that I was some kind of two-wheeled mobile police officer patrolling the bridge like the old Berlin Wall – and wanted to see his papers.

Bloody hell – ID papers for travel from Fife to Midlothian? I know the Jocks have now got home rule but this was taking security too far.

Luckily I was joined by a Scots gentleman about 5' 2" tall and weighing in the region of 16 st. At first glance he looked like a beer barrel with little legs attached. Our foreign friend saw his opportunity and scuttled off, leaving me with me to deal with my next challenger.

We exchanged greetings and I learned that my human beer keg had spent the best part of his life in the Army but had been discharged due to a major heart problem.

He told me that every day he marched over the bridge and then marched back again. I was tempted to ask him if he had ever met the Grand old Duke of York, but decided against it as the fingers of his hands resembled a pound of Melton Mowbray's best pork sausages. He was also wearing an assortment of rings, the largest being one with an old guinea coin attached – experience telling me that all men wearing those are slightly unbalanced.

The good news was that, after a swift four minute lesson from me, he understood how to press the button on my camera while at the same time pointing it in the general direction of my choice – namely at me. Two separate lessons completed in less than five minutes – we were motoring. Soon the operation was completed and I went on to phase two of my plan – seeking precise directions to Kelty.

Bad news. While my pocket rocket pal had seen active service in many parts of the world (his quote not mine), he was at a loss to pinpoint a specific town within six miles of his own home.

My stay on the Bridge was fast resembling a United Nations Congress meeting as next to join me was a 50-something school teacher from the Home Counties. She was a cyclist and had just alighted at Waverley railway station and was cycling to her home in Dunfermline. I pleaded with her to save me and she promised to show me the way.

I thanked the walking advert for McEwan's heavy for his input, hoping the sincerity in my voice was roughly in line with the assistance he had provided and he waddled off to complete his day's route march.

Crossing the Bridge in tow of my latest friend was not a problem but the steep B917 road that was waiting for us on the other side certainly was. I was too proud to ask my middle-aged female pace setter to slow down so gambled about three days' of energy to stay with her to the top. We eventually arrived at the summit and she shot off left, leaving me with precise instructions on how to find Kelty.

As instructed I carried on, through the Hill O'Beath, past the magnificent life-size bronze statue of the legendary Scottish footballer Jim Baxter and on towards Kelty three miles distant. It was now well after six in the evening and the 72 miles I had travelled felt more like 172 due to most of them being ridden in heavy rain.

Then I punctured.

Early evening, nine hours on the road, soaked and knackered and I punctured.

I set up camp on a small grassy roundabout but spotted a house close by with an empty carport. It looked ideal for a shelter and makeshift pit stop. Sadly, there was no reply to my knock at the door, so I returned dejected to my own magic roundabout.

All cyclists will know the irritation of changing an inner tube.

First of all, it is always the rear wheel that has blown, necessitating fiddling with the dérailleur and getting filthy hands. Prior to that, both panniers have to be removed and the bike turned upside down. Finally, and this is the hard bit with a tired mind, the memory has to be good to recall where all the various nuts and bolts were dropped in the deep grass in order for assembly to recommence.

I didn't think that my spirit or mood could worsen when my mobile sparked into life. It was Bill Tomlinson the head of the Derbyshire Children's Holiday Centre, a charity that provides holidays for under- privileged children. It was the chosen charity of the Derby County Former Players' Association and the one that I had generated £5,500 for in sponsorship.

Bill had been a fantastic support leading up to my ride and very appreciative of my efforts to raise much needed cash for the kids, but at that precise moment in time I did not feel inclined to enter into idle chit-chat about the day's events. And that is putting it slightly more politely than I was feeling. With a promise to call him back later I excused myself, uttered another oath and completed the repair.

Within 10 minutes I was outside Lochfitty Cottage in Lassodie near Kingseat and Kelty saying hello to Norman Woolley. And was I pleased to see him.

Norman was just what I needed at that moment, absolutely superb. Not only did he take my wet gear away to launder, he also dried my cycling shoes. Then he wiped down my bike and oiled the chain plus any other part that apparently required oil. He followed that by telephoning the Hideaway restaurant near Dunfermline and persuaded them to keep the kitchen open an extra 30 minutes so I could get some dinner. Finally, he topped all that by driving me to and from the restaurant.

What a great man and wonderful host – and there was still more to come.

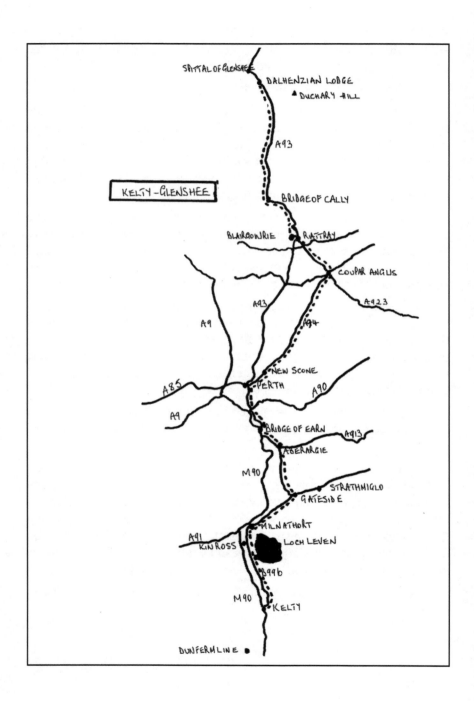

Day 11
Kelty to Glenshee

PRIOR to leaving my Lochfitty Cottage B&B to continue with my journey north into the Cairngorms, I had two errands to complete. One was purchasing some more inner tubes for my bike and the other, to seek medical assistance for my troublesome hip that the Peebles pharmacies had so neatly sidestepped.

Norman came to my rescue again and we motored into Dunfermline to the Asda Superstore that housed a pharmacy. I asked the young assistant if I could speak with the pharmacist. Moving 15 feet to her right she spoke briefly with her colleague before returning and telling me that the pharmacist wouldn't be free for at least 30 minutes.

I politely persisted, explaining that a 10 second glance at my hip would suffice and allow her to prescribe the appropriate ointment and dressing. Neither the assistant nor her pharmacist were for turning, so I purchased basic lint dressing and tape and moved on, reasoning that my self-diagnosis and subsequent purchase of lint would absorb the fluid seeping from my wound.

Leaving the store I happened to pass the store's information desk and what did I see?

Yes, you've got it in one – only the prima-donna of a pharmacist leaning on the desk, having a natter with her colleague.

From a distance, I watched for fully two minutes as they, no doubt, exchanged views on the previous night's episodes of Coronation Street and EastEnders.

My, they were having fun. It was clear they enjoyed each other's company – and in work time too. How could the lazy sods behave like that when there were customers, who paid their salaries, waiting for a smidgeon of good 'old-fashioned' service in order to ride more comfortably to John O'Groats?

Being of a polite disposition, I said nothing, merely fixed her with one of my meanest stares, at the same time promising myself, that en route to Perth, I would mentally prepare a stiff complaint letter to the chief executive of Asda UK with a copy to the president of Walmart. Nobody messes with me when it comes to service quality.

Sure enough, later in the day the letter was duly composed, and boy was it a strong one, no punches pulled.

Sadly, by the time I reached Glenshee that evening I had forgotten its content. It never was sent.

We were soon in and out of Halfords with the inner tubes I required and back at Normans for my bike and the next stage of my journey. After Norman had fixed my faltering odometer I waved him good-bye, glad that a 'saint' had been waiting for me at the end of my arduous day riding up from the borders.

It was 10.10 a.m. when I left, the weather overcast, with a hint of rain. Norman had re-written my route to Glenshee suggesting initially I take the B996, a road that ran parallel with the M90 almost to Perth.

The road was smooth and undulating with no major challenges, and I set a good pace for Kelty, Kinross, Loch Leven and Milnathort before turning on to the A91 to pass through Gateside and Strathmiglo.

The problem was, I didn't want to be in Strathmiglo. I should have been nowhere near Strathmiglo – it was 5 miles too far. I should have taken the A912 north when I hit Gateside.

There was nothing I could do except turn round and ride back the 5 miles I had come. What a pain, 10 wasted miles – not a good move when added to the late departure time. What I couldn't understand was how I had missed my turn.

Eventually I was back in Gateside and saw the turn that I should have taken. Coming at it from a different angle the A912 signpost was loud and clear. However, coming from the other direction it had been conveniently obscured by a parked police van housing a speed camera.

To date I had not been overly impressed by the efficiency of the 'polis.' On Sunday I had been allowed to ride eight miles down a motorway and today they were masking an important road sign while endeavouring to make a few quid out of the pockets of errant drivers. Add those two shortcomings to the fact they were letting overseas maniacs loose on the most important bridge in their country and you will see why I was unimpressed.

I hurried up the A road north, averaging a very handsome 18 miles an hour, trying to pick up lost time – Aberargie and the Bridge of Earn both flying by as I closed in on Perth.

Following Perth, my route was taking me out on to the A94 to New Scone before diverting on to the busy A923 at Coupar Angus for Blairgowrie and Rattray.

At Coupar Angus I stopped at a bakery for a coffee, éclair and meringue and qualified for one of the most unorthodox entries in the Guinness Book of Records ever. I'm not proud of what I am about to tell you, but as the saying goes: 'If needs must'.

With the shop empty and staff otherwise engaged, by standing bolt upright next to the flapjacks, I managed to ease my hand down the back of my cycling shorts and smear a large dollop of Vaseline on my arse. It had been troubling me for some time and was demanding attention. Let me make it quite clear, I would not normally select the retail area of a rather up-market bakery as a mini operating theatre, but in mitigation there were no customers or staff and there was a glass screen separating my greasy bum from the loaves and confectionery. The most important thing was, that my backside immediately took a turn for the better and gave me a trouble-free ride up Glenshee.

Every cloud has a silver lining I suppose – I know my arse had.

Before I left I did have fun with the staff. I asked them if I could guess how many doughnuts she was putting in the bag could I have one? She told me that if I could guess correctly I could have both of them.

I just missed out with my guess of three.

Up until now the day had been very kind to me barring the mistake I had made at Gateside – all this was to change however when I left Blairgowrie, the A93 all the way to the Bridge of Cally and beyond being one long steep drawn out crawl.

I was entering the Cairngorms, part of the Grampian Mountains, and they were giving me notice of the severity I could expect over the next two days.

Sadly, walking formed a part of my recreational activities as I pushed deeper into the mountains, I was in a 'no-man's-land' with the Forest of Alyth to the east and the soaring peak of Deuchary Hill to the west.

The mileage from the Bridge of Cally to my B&B at Dalhenzean Lodge, south of Glenshee was less than 20 miles but it was a hard 20 miles, especially when a part of it was on foot. I had been working out my percentages all through the day and had estimated that if I maintained an average speed of 12 mph I would arrive at my destination at around 4.30 p.m. This proved to be unerringly accurate for at 4.45 p.m. I saw the gates of my host , Mike Purdie's lodge and I knew another day was behind me.

Mike and Joyce Purdie have a marvellously spacious 300-year-old home, a former hunting lodge, that looks out over the Cairngorms, two miles south of the Spittal of Glenshee. All around them lies the Cateran Trail, a 60 mile hiking route along drove roads and ancient tracks originally frequented by cattle thieves who raided the area between the middle ages and the 17th century. An ideal summers walk - for hikers with 'attitude'.

Mike, a former Wing Commander in the RAF is quite a character. His service career lasted 26 years and during that time he headed up the 100 Squadron, flying Canberras. While not seeing active service, he toured with a reconnaissance squadron in Germany during the Cold war when actual war was a distinct possibility. Mike enjoys talking about his career, so if you are an aircraft fanatic, Mike's your man.

He was also a very proud man and displayed his flying suit and dress uniform alongside Joyce's father's Scots Guards dress uniform, on pegs in the hall. I felt it rude if I failed to make a contribution to the pageantry, so hung my hi-viz jacket and cycling helmet there too to complete the set, the fluorescent yellow setting off the red and blue of the other uniforms rather nicely I thought.

I can only assume that Mike felt slightly inferior when he spotted my dashing colours, for when I came down from my bath my jacket and helmet and been moved to another location. Isn't it strange how grown men can be so envious of a brightly coloured riding jacket? And isn't it sad how an inferiority complex can take such a hold?

Just after 6.00 p.m. he drove me up to the Spittal of Glenshee Hotel for my dinner. Glen Shee is taken from the Gaelic `'shith' meaning Glen of the Fairies, but as I was to find out next day, it was anything but.

The hotel is of Scandinavian design rebuilt in 1959, replacing the original one that dated back to 961 AD. That one was destroyed by fire but I reassured myself there would not be a repeat performance as I sat staring at the roaring log fire while sinking my first pint of Boddingtons in the deserted bar.

My mind wandered as I looked out over the stunning Highlands, and I made a mental note to research the history of the Munros that I had spasmodically read about in books before venturing on my trip.

They are named after Sir Hugh Munro, the first man to climb all 283 of them. Now over 4,000 others have achieved this feat, the current record to scale them all being 40 days, an average of seven every day. I reflected that I had struggled to climb up Mike's stairs seven times at the Lodge, never mind a 3,000 feet plus Munro.

Corbetts, that number 221, are mountains between 2,500 and 3,000 ft, with Grahams bringing up the rear at over 2,000 ft – 224 of them.

With the aid of a map I spun 360 degrees in my seat and spotted one Munro, Glas Maol at 3,556 ft, five Corbetts and a Graham – not a bad day's work in less than five minutes.

I have to admit that, with the bar being empty, my dinner not ready and being alone, I was ever so slightly bored so I idled away my time and let my mind wander.

How many Corbetts could I recall?

Ronnie was easy, quickly followed by Harry H. of Steptoe fame. Then came Gentleman Jim Corbett the legendary boxer. He once knocked out John L. Sullivan in the 21st round of a heavyweight fight in New York in 1892. Bit like a boxing equivalent of a penalty shoot out I thought.

Harry was my fourth choice but far more people will remember him as making good money from shoving his hand up Sooty's arse on a daily basis. Hard to believe isn't it, he made a good living, hand covered in crap, while talking to a glove puppet who just nodded before assaulting him with a toy wand. He never did learn.

Few people know that Harry's mother's brother was the great fish fryer Harry Ramsden.

Harry Corbett's son Matthew took over Sooty's anal passage from his Dad after years of sexually assaulting Sweep (in those days things like that were hushed up weren't they?), before selling the whole family business for a few million pounds.

Seems to me to be a classic case of one set of piles to another.

Good value, eh? Not only do you read about an old fart riding from Land's End to John O'Groats, you also get a celebrity history lesson for your money.

Over the main course of my meal I moved on to Grahams but could only recall three. George 'stroller' Graham, a footballer with Aston Villa,

Chelsea, Arsenal and Scotland in the 60s and 70s , Herrol Graham, the boxer, and finally good old Billy Graham, the world-famous evangelist.

I was getting tired by the time I moved on to the Munros, failing miserably by only recounting Janet Munro, an English actress from 50 years back. Disgracefully I resorted to cheating by inserting Matt Monro, the singer of the Bond film theme tune *From Russia with Love*, followed by the lovely Marylyn.

My mental gymnastics had got me through my dinner and halfway down my second 'Boddies', and I smiled to myself for playing the silly game. There I was, after nearly 11 days of total solitude going stir crazy, or the cyclist's equivalent.

Thank goodness I didn't take on the hills-guessing game. Now first comes Benny ...

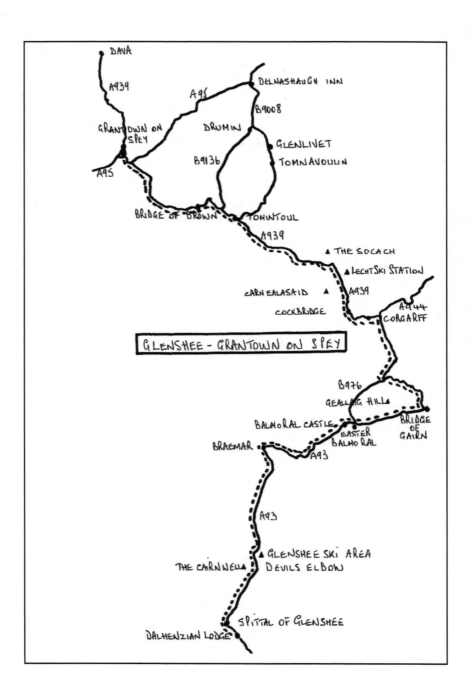

DAVA

A939

DELNASHAUGH INN

A95

B9008

GRANTOWN ON SPEY

DRUMIN

GLENLIVET

B9136

TOMNAVOULIN

A95

BRIDGE OF BROWN

TOMINTOUL

A939

▲ THE SOCACH

▲ LECHT SKI STATION

CARN EALASAID ▲

A939

COCKBRIDGE

A944

CORGARFF

GLENSHEE - GRANTOWN ON SPEY

B976

GEALLAIG HILL ▲

BALMORAL CASTLE

EASTER BALMORAL

BRIDGE OF GAIRN

BRAEMAR

A93

A93

▲ GLENSHEE SKI AREA

THE CAIRNWELL ▲

DEVILS ELBOW

SPITTAL OF GLENSHEE

DALHENZIAN LODGE

Day 12
Glenshee to Grantown-on-Spey

I WILL never forget Mike Purdie's final words to me as I photographed him with his wife , Joyce, at their Lodge gate before I left.

In a beautiful cut-glass accent that only a wing commander with a lifetime in the RAF could produce, Mike said: 'Do me a favour old boy, give me a quick bell when you arrive in Grantown.'

Little did I know why Mike was making that request but very soon it was going to be abundantly clear to me.

I left the Dalhenzean Lodge at 9.30 a.m., but not before Mike, Joyce and another of Mike's guests had given me a generous donation for my charity. As Mike wryly remarked: 'The one and only time that I have ever paid someone to stay with me'.

My target for the day was Grantown-on-Spey, a ride of 72 miles taking me via the well-known tourist resorts of Braemar, the River Dee, Balmoral Castle and Tomintoul. It promised to be an eventful experience.

The early stages of my journey took me north on the A93, past the Spittal of Glenshee Hotel where I had dined the night before and up the Glen towards the notorious 'Devils Elbow'.

It was an education in itself to survey the road ahead.

On a dank, grey day I could just about see it as it climbed the five miles and a height of 1,100 feet, before disappearing from sight over the summit. While not being the steepest incline I had encountered, its length, together with the severity, would turn out to be a challenge that would test my stamina to the full.

I cannot say the road was pretty in any sense of the word – sure there were high mountains all around me, many still harbouring snow in their crevices (well it was June), but the weather, combined with the monotony of the long climb, meant that it was sensible to mentally switch off and just get through the tedium with my brain in neutral.

As I rode I noticed that there were many dead hares lying by the roadside – surely not all of them could have been the result of accidents? I could only assume that many had lost the will to live and had dived in front of a passing vehicle. Either that or they were particularly bad at their version of the game 'chicken'.

At regular intervals of 20 yards, wooden poles 10ft high had been erected on both sides of the road, a winter assistance to snow ploughs when road clearance was necessary. An excellent example I thought, of keeping the show, not the snow, on the road.

One feature along the road impressed me greatly. From the sides of the mountain, every 100 yards or so, were small waterfalls dropping through a series of wooden boxes channelling the excess rainwater from on high before gathering it in deep ditches to drain away. It gave a very tidy and organised feel to the scene and no doubt helped stem land erosion.

I seemed to be climbing forever, the steepest sections being conquered in short bursts; a 100-yard ride followed by one minute's rest – then repeated. And so it went on. For anyone with a low attention span the climb would have driven them crazy, the sameness being soul destroying.

I was able to maintain my discipline though by focussing on the fact that after 45–50 minutes of hard graft I would be at Devil's Elbow, a famous landmark a mile south of the Glenshee ski station at the summit of the Cairnwell Pass. I took little consolation that the main road I was on was the highest in the UK, one that rose to a total height of 3,100 ft.

The Devil's Elbow originally was a double hairpin bend with a gradient of 33 per cent (a one foot in three climb), so steep that it is rumoured that Nepalese Sherpa's once visited it, took a look, and returned home shaking their heads in disbelief. They had obviously decided that Everest was an easier stroll.

Now the road bypasses the worst of the gradient, but make no mistake, it is still one hell of a climb. With great pride I can say that I conquered Devil's Elbow – without walking.

The Glenshee ski station based at the summit looked a little forlorn in the damp, overcast conditions. With no snow around its buildings, no sun to sharpen or brighten its redundant equipment, the UK's most extensive ski and snowboarding centre - featuring 21 lifts and 36 runs, two of them black - looked forgotten, tired, and deserted.

I was glad to move on, especially as my toil from below the Spittal to the top meant that I could now freewheel down the Glen to Braemar.

However, even that brought mixed feelings. The effort of getting to the summit had made me sweat, the only good news of the day to date, but the descent back to civilisation also brought its problems: four downhill miles at 40 mph in freezing conditions being a high penalty to pay. I was wet through and frozen.

I came into Braemar past the Golf Club and reflected on how many days a year the course was open in officially the coldest and wettest inhabited village in the UK. Records show that temperatures hit a low of -27°C in January 1982, and it crossed my mind that June 2010 was running that record just a wee bit too close.

It has its fair share of precipitation too, 36 inches of it on average every year, so at first glance if you were cold blooded and didn't like wet weather, Braemar would not feature high on your list of places to 'must see'.

On a positive note however, the village's other claim to fame is the Highland Gathering held in September and attended by the Queen and Prince Philip. Balmoral Castle is only a 15 minute bus ride away and is probably free for visiting pensioners from London – all helpful in these economically stressful times.

A friend of mine who clearly has something against all those who originate from north of the border sent me an unkind text message in response to me telling him that I was in Braemar. He reckoned that the Highland Games organisers were trying to add a charity pancake competition to the event. They were going to provide the pans and ingredients but had to cancel when too many tossers turned up for the heats. I find that so unfair, don't you – surely they could have found more batter mix.

After my decidedly cold descent from the summit of Glenshee I was in need of a cup of coffee, so I locked my bike, unclipped my panniers and entered Braemar's best hotel.

It took five seconds or so, possibly six, for me to realise that the cavalry twill trouser and tweed skirt brigade did not wish to welcome me with open arms. In fact, I got the distinct impression that they were unsure exactly what had just walked into the hotel foyer.

Had they never seen a man wearing a 'bunch of bananas' black cycling helmet, fluorescent yellow rain jacket, black Lycra shorts and grey cycling shoes, complete with cleats? It appeared not. For that matter, neither had the staff.

I was quick to take advantage of their hesitance and had bought a coffee and sat myself down in a tartan patterned deep armchair long before the gaping mouths of the patrons had returned to neutral.

Furthermore, my panniers were open, map spread and I was deep in concentrated thought planning the next stage of my ride. It was far too late for the front desk receptionist to summon the duty manager and kick me out. Anyway, he was no doubt undertaking his regular performance review with 'the fit-looking' young chambermaid in the linen cupboard on the third floor – a 'Don't Disturb' sign no doubt hanging on the door.

I eked out my stay for fully 20 minutes until I felt my point had been made. I even got the feeling that I was slowly being accepted as part of the furniture, judging by some of the watery smiles that were spreading across the lined faces of the guests. Whether a brisk 'Good morning' would have followed within a day or two is hard to guess, suffice to say that I was no longer being treated like an alien.

I often look back at that little cameo in the Fife Arms Hotel in Braemar and wonder if the chambermaid received top marks for her bedmaking skills?

With my temperature back to a more normal 98.6°F I set off up the A93, through Balmoral Forest, in the general direction of Aberdeen, knowing that, way short of the granite city, I would shoot due north for Grantown-on-Spey.

Between Braemar and Balmoral Castle I marvelled at the road surface while simultaneously wondering if the quality that I could feel beneath my tyres would have been up to the same standards if our reigning monarch had not had a summer holiday home in the vicinity. It was good enough to accommodate a Formula 1 Grand Prix car, a Roller, a Bentley, even a carriage and four.

I was now riding through woodland alongside the River Dee and spotted a fly fisherman, knee deep in his waders, casting his rod, his ever-watchful 'ghillie' on the bank guarding his master's flask and sandwiches. I wanted to approach him and ask if his well-heeled boss had caught any flies but rejected the thought after I had convinced myself that a) it was a cheap and unfunny line and b) 'rod man' looked just a teeny bit Greek. Of course, it could have been a trick of the light but I consoled myself by taking a photograph when he was casting – and do you know, I caught the action shot perfectly?

Scrambling back to the road I continued on, only taking a small detour to the main gate of Balmoral Castle for another photo opportunity. Viewing the photograph later, I saw that I had cleverly obscured the main gate with my thumb – either that or there was some dastardly clever security operation at work.

For some unexplained reason I missed the left turn for Tomintoul, riding on obliviously until reaching Ballater. There I saw two signs both pointing to the A93 to Aberdeen but going in different directions. To this day I have been unable to solve that little conundrum, but fortunately they did alert me to the fact that I was going the wrong way.

Not wanting to retrace my steps back to the B976 that I had missed near Balmoral, I rang Mike Purdie back at the Dalhenzean Lodge to seek advice. Immediately he put me right, explaining that there was a cut through at the Bridge of Gairn that would take me through Candacraig and back on to the Tomintoul road.

Although the road was steep, it was manageable and I was soon back on course, that is until I felt my rear tyre slowly deflating. I stopped and pumped it up, but a further deflation told me it was a puncture and a new inner tube required.

I was out in the foothills of the East Cairngorm mountains, overlooked by Geallaig Hill, rising 2,500 ft up to my right. It had started to drizzle, I was way behind time and I had punctured. I was not happy, even though deep down I knew I was fortunate to have only incurred three punctures in over 800 miles. Little did I know, that within five minutes I would have a totally justifiable reason to be as miserable as sin.

The panniers came off, the bike was upturned, the offending tube removed, replaced by one of Halfords' best. All that was needed was the tyre re-inflated and I would be on my way.

Sadly I was wrong. Before even 5 lb of pressure could be applied the pump broke into two pieces in my hand. Well and truly broken.

I was now stranded, out in the wilds, completely helpless. Me, a bike, but no air.

I have to concede that I came out with words that I would not use in front of my grandchildren, wife, mates that I drink and share crude jokes with, or even the foul-mouthed yob that I had once had a run in with on the Northern Line underground in 1973. Even wild animals covered their ears.

The bike, panniers, surrounding wilderness, and especially the pump, got both barrels. It would be fair to say that I was a trifle disappointed.

I returned to earth and thought. It was approaching 2.30 p.m., I was in the middle of nowhere and I was immobile – oh, and I was cold and wet.

What could I do now?

Looking around me, more for divine intervention that anything else, I spotted a building some 200 yards away across a field. It was difficult to tell whether it was a store shed or a small house? I began my trek across the sodden meadow still clutching my pump – both bits, but hadn't reached halfway when out of the building came a person who I can only describe as 'Spock-like'.

He was of average height and build, about 70 years of age, had a completely bald, pink head, pointed nose and elephant-sized ears.

'Can I help ye?' he shouted, in an accent that would be impossible to put in writing.

I thought to myself, cut the sob story and tell it like it is.

'I've punctured and my pump broke as I was inflating the new inner tube.' I replied, hoping that my succinct summary would be enough for him to grasp an understanding of my predicament.

In a million years you would not believe what he said next. No, make that two million.

'Och, I'm a keen cyclist myself and I have a hand pump in the garage, I'll be right over'.

I swear that I looked up into the grey leaden sky above, ignored the rain beating on my face and mouthed: 'Thank you'.

Within a few minutes he had made me roadworthy and politely asked where I was heading. I told him Grantown-on-Spey.

My answer generated a facial wince and a sharp intake of breath. If I may say so, it was a very good impersonation of Paul Gascoigne's face, seconds after being grabbed in the wedding tackle by Vinnie Jones following a contretemps at White Hart Lane in 1987.

'Have you no heard of the Lecht laddie,' he said.

'Er no, should I have?'

'Aye, it's always mentioned on Terry Wogan's radio show when the weather is bad in these parts,' continued Spock, 'Wogan is always saying that Mrs McDonald will be sweeping the snow off her doorstep on the Lecht.'

He went on to explain in frightening detail the conditions I would find on my route up to the Lecht ski station still some distance ahead, finishing with a final word of discouragement: 'And you won't get up the hill a mile yonder either, you'll have to walk there too.'

By this stage I wasn't sure whether to thank him for his kindness and accurate directions or let my down tyre again, break his pump, drop to my knees and say: 'Any chance of a cup of tea?'

Rightly or wrongly I chose the former and went on my way, thankful that this strange-looking, but warm-hearted man, had given me a 50/50 chance of survival even if it was for no more than two hours.

He was not wrong about the Lecht, neither was he wrong about the steep climb leading to the steep climb to the Lecht.

Let me first take the first climb, the one through Corgarff and Cock Bridge, but before I do let me remind you how I scaled Glenshee. You may recall that I rode 100 yards, rested for one minute and rode another 100 yards, and so on.

This was slightly different although the yardages remained the same. So steep was the climb that I walked 100 yards, rested for one minute and walked another 100 yards, and so on.

Yes, you've spotted it: 'walk' substituted for 'rode'. As master of the understatement I will summarise by saying: 'It was quite hard'.

Now, add to the severity of the incline a chill wind that was reducing air temperatures to similar levels to those you would find in your average domestic fridge's ice-box, rain that was cascading down sideways, and a cloud base that restricted my view to less than 80 yards and you will be about 50 per cent towards empathising with the situation I was in.

Listen, I am not looking for sympathy, or trying to make out I am some kind of hero who has just scaled Everest in a tee-shirt, Speedos and desert boots, all I am endeavouring to do is paint a picture of my predicament. And in all honesty, having just re-read the above, 50 per cent towards empathising may be a trifle high. After answering my prayers by finding a pump in the wilderness, the man upstairs was testing me.

But, when there is no way back there is only one way to go – forward.

Chin close to the handlebars and taking a wide girth to avoid my panniers rubbing my thigh, I started to push and push and push. The first hill was gradually conquered, followed by a brief riding period, then more walking, every yard taking me closer to the distant summit.

All I can say about the climb is that it was character-building.

Not only was it steeper and longer than the previous challenge, the higher I climbed the more conditions worsened. Visibility dropped, wind chill increased, and rain intensified. It was excruciatingly miserable, made worse by the fact that there was no one but me there. I could not even be motivated by the distance behind me that I had climbed, as that had long disappeared from view in the mountain mist.

After what seemed like an eternity I eventually arrived at the summit.

The Lecht, famous for the many mentions on Breakfast with Wogan, famous for its 20 assorted runs and 15 lifts, and now famous, with me anyway, for taking me to the limits of my human endurance.

And do you know? Up at the ski station there was still nobody about, just me. It was totally desolate. Nobody to nod a friendly acknowledgement to, nowhere to get a warm drink, nothing except for a few deserted buildings and a series of stark metal robot-looking pylons that, one day soon, would again be carrying skiers via chairlifts to the top of the slopes.

It was a strange, almost out-of-body experience to be there. The vile weather, deserted ski apparatus, solitude, exhaustion, all adding to the peculiar feeling that I had done something different compared to anything

I had ever done before.

Even running marathons could not come close, for with them there was always company around to share woes.

This was different. For something like an hour and a half I had fought the environment alone, with no words of encouragement from accompanying friends or family, just me against whatever the elements threw.

I like to think that, on reflection, it was a score draw. Neither side had backed off and both had made their point.

As with the descent from Glenshee to Braemar, the drop from the Lecht into Tomintoul was a cold and terrifying experience. The road was wet, visibility poor, and, at speeds in excess of 40 miles per hour, there was always the danger of a spill. Chilled to the marrow and with spectacles blurred by rain it was difficult to decide whether coming down or going up was the preferable option. I decided on neither – both being inhumane.

But like all good stories, there was a happy ending – the road flattening out and the magical words of 'Tomintoul' appearing below 'Welcome to'.

Tomintoul, with its population of 350 soon came into view and I found a coffee shop that was still open. It was full of mature German motorcyclists, all of them warmed by the numerous coffees they had probably consumed.

I must have looked a sorry sight, standing in the doorway, panniers in hand, bottom lip trembling and knees knocking, but they politely ignored me and it was left to the lady serving to say: 'Want a warm love?'

'Good start,' I thought and nodded. Was she the old-fashioned type who still favoured a fast massage to get the blood flowing? Was she cold too? Did she want one? For a fleeting second I thought it was pay-back time after the cruelty inflicted by the Lecht.

Sadly, I was still in a post-Lecht traumatic hallucination – I had got too far ahead of myself – and her.

She switched the convector heater on above the door and I felt a wave of warm air encase my body. If this is the only option on offer I'll have it I thought.

I wanted to stay there for the rest of my life but restricted it to a couple of minutes, the need for caffeine taking over from the cold.

'Got far to go?' she said.

I wanted to say: 'I haven't a bloody clue,' but instead replied: 'I'll let you know after I have made contact with my bed and breakfast landlady in Grantown.'

This I duly did and was told that I was 14 miles from Grantown, but to brace myself for the steep hill coming out of the 'Brig O'Broon'. This warning mystified me until the lady who served me my coffee politely pointed to the place on my map that said, The Bridge of Brown.

Reluctantly, I left the coffee shop at 5 p.m. for my final leg of the day to Grantown, my one consolation being that in a shade over an hour I would be warm and dry and away from the spiteful slopes of the Cairngorms.

I had neither the time nor the inclination to read about Tomintoul and the famed Whisky Trail that traces its way through Pufftown, Keith and Tomnavoulin. No time to glance at the Glenlivet Estate or try a wee dram of Glenfiddich or Macallan. And for that matter, no time to sample any one of the 60 single malts that were distilled in and around Speyside.

All I wanted to do was ride up the path of Dunallan House in Woodside Avenue, Grantown-on-Spey and say hello to Jayne and David Graham.

It was early evening when my wish came true and within 15 minutes of arriving I was lounging in a hot bath, recalling the most adventurous and challenging day of my ride so far. In all probability it was the best bath that I had ever had in my life, even better that the one I had, in my dreams, with Barbara Windsor in 1961, when I was 16.

Mind you, thinking back that was also a bloody good one.

Back in my room, I caught the last few seconds of the TV weather girl. Maybe it was just for Scottish viewers only, maybe I misunderstood her accent, I can't be sure, but I think I heard her say that she was expecting eight inches that night. Not with a face like that I thought.

David recommended the pub 100 yards up the road for my evening meal, advising that their pie, peas and chips should not be ignored. Suddenly I realised that the only footwear I possessed, other than my cycling shoes, were trainers that were now sodden from the miles of walking I had done in the rain. With no other options available I had accepted that my feet would remain wet. That is, until David noticed and stepped in, handing me a pair of his own trainers for me to wear.

Let's just analyse that gesture for a moment. If I had been staying in a 5-star hotel, at a considerably higher cost to that which I was paying to Jayne and David, would the hotel's front-of house manager lend me a pair of his trainers for the evening? I think not. Yet here was a man I had never met before in my life providing me with footwear in order for me to have a comfortable evening down at his local. I rest my case.

My evening got even better when I entered the Craig Bar and got talking to the landlady. She hailed from Wimbledon and had remained in Grantown after her husband died. She was good company and an even better cook, the steak and kidney pie, peas and chips complementing the three pints of local ale I demolished.

In Biblical terms it was a case of 'out of darkness cometh light'. Take my word for it – the sun was metaphorically shining when I left the Craig Bar at 10 p.m. that night. Not only had I been fed and watered well, enjoyed excellent company, I had only been charged for my meal, the beer being with the compliments of the house.

For the second time on my ride the pub landlady had been an angel.

My day was almost over but not before I remembered to put a call through to Mike Purdie, my previous night's landlord in Glenshee. It was late but I got through.

'Apologies for the late hour Mike, but I can report that I arrived in

Grantown at 6.30. By the way, why were you so adamant I call you when I arrived?'

He replied: 'You went over the Lecht didn't you?'

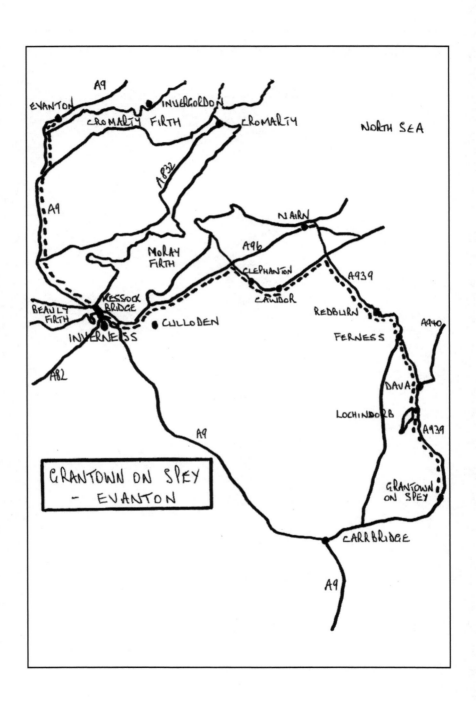

Day 13
Grantown-on-Spey to Evanton

WITH my task for the day the short 58 mile ride to Evanton I was in no hurry to leave Grantown and, following breakfast, stayed for some time chatting to Jane and David. Both were keen skiers and mountain bike enthusiasts and seemed to have a perfect life; Jane running the B&B, with David undertaking his duties as a part-time fireman. Their life sounded idyllic, skiing in winter and biking in summer, daily guests being the only mild intrusion.

David came up trumps again for me, this time mending my pump, so I was able to leave them, confident that I could face another puncture, or any other challenge that required a bicycle pump emitting air.

My route was idiot-proof, the mileage low, and it was after 10.00 a.m. when I said good-bye and set off up the A939 towards Dava.

Initially my plan had been to travel through Inverness, ride across the Black Isle to Cromarty, overnight there and then take the short ferry crossing to Balnapaling. I would then meet the A9 that would take me all the way up the east coast to the end of my ride.

Unfortunately, about two months before I left home I received a call from the Manager of my Cromarty Hotel advising me that the summer ferry schedule had been delayed due to the late arrival of a new boat. I would not be able to cross the Cromarty Firth.

A rescue plan was soon at hand when Cotswolds-based Nigel Methley, a cycling coach who rode LEJOG frequently, recommended that I stay inland from Inverness, ride straight up the middle of Scotland to Bettyhill before turning east to follow the north coast to John O'Groats. That would enable me to spend a night at the Crask Inn, his all-time favourite night stop.

So today's evening stay would be at the Novar Arms in Evanton, a hop and a skip above Inverness. Before leaving my B&B, David told me the terrain to Evanton was flat, so I was looking forward to a comfortable stress-free day.

There was a cold north-east wind blowing in my face when I left Grantown, necessitating me wearing tracksuit bottoms. After two weeks in the saddle it was the first time the weather was cold and dry.

The A939 over the peat bogs to Dava and Nairn was fast in spite of the headwind, the 22 miles until the B9101 turn south-west for Cawdor being covered in well under two hours.

The landscape across Dava Moor and into Ferness and Redburn was wild land without much cultivation – better still it was, as David suggested, relatively flat and I was able to relax and enjoy the ride – the trials, tribulations and challenges of the Lecht behind me.

Today was a new chapter and within 24 hours I had pushed the previous day's experience to the back of my mind. Looking forward with anticipation was the key to success – not back with regret.

From Cawdor, the road swung north-west into Clephanton and within 15 minutes I had met the main A96 that runs between Inverness and Aberdeen. The wind was directly behind me now and my odometer was telling me that I was travelling at 18 mph even though I was exerting very little pressure on the pedals. Oh, the joy.

Past the airport I raced, on the final 10 miles sprint to Inverness, the aircraft movements providing a welcome sideshow as I bowled along. On my left I saw a sign for the Culloden battlefield so stopped and asked a passer-by to take a photograph of me for posterity.

154

I had heard about the Battle of Culloden but knew no detail.

Further research revealed that it was the final pitched battle of the Jacobite rebellion, fought in 1745, when the Jacobite forces of Charles Edward Stuart fought against the Duke of Cumberland's men who were loyal to the British Government and the reigning House of Hanover. Not much had changed there then in over 250 years, the Scots and English are still knocking 10 bags of crap out of each other, physically and politically.

The battle only lasted an hour, although it is reported that 2000 were killed, 90 per cent of the Jacobites. It crossed my mind that most of the English forces must have been Millwall football supporters, but reading on I found that the Duke had called on troops from as far a field as the lowlands of Scotland (traitors to you and me), Ulster, Austria, plus a few stray Hessians – a German regiment hired by the Government. Lucky the battle only lasted an hour – if it had gone to extra time, as in 1966 at Wembley, the Hessians would have caved in.

Austria also seems like a long way to travel to me – the outskirts of Vienna to the north of Scotland for an hour's scrap. Maybe they were on a camping holiday in the area and went over the wall to see what all the noise was about? We'll never know.

I would be willing to bet that the most famous spoken line in English football commentary was coined at Culloden and paraphrased by Kenneth Wolstenholme: 'The Jocks think it's all over – it is now'.

The rest, as they say, is history.

It had been a perfect start to the day, trouble-free, and I was already well over halfway through my day's mileage. I would be in Evanton earlier than planned.

It was when I was standing high above Inverness photographing Kessock Bridge a little hiccup occurred – the battery on my camera expired. Thomas, my son, had assured me that it would be good for the whole trip and more, but he was wrong – it was even more lifeless than many of my infrequent appearances for the Rams, way back in the 60s.

With lunchtime beckoning I made the decision to stop at the local out- of-town Tesco Superstore for a sandwich and coffee and purchase another battery. While the catering side of the store satisfied my desires (the chicken and salad sandwich and latte coffee come highly recommended), their photographic section came up short. The country's leading retailer had drawn a blank: no battery and no charger, their only advice being to call into photographic experts, Jessops, in town.

Jessops was easily tracked down in Union Street and the rather surly, but in all fairness, overworked sales assistant was able to satisfy my request – she had a charger for the battery at a cost of £30.00. As I only wanted a quick burst of power, having a perfectly good charger safe and sound at home, I cheekily asked if she would insert the charger into the rear end of my camera for an hour or so for a £15.00 'cash-in-hand' drink?

Whether she thought this was a mystery shopper ruse or not, I will never know as she held her ground, only relenting slightly by saying that if I bought a charger she would kick-start life into my camera, with the electricity being with the compliments of Jessops.

I was a beaten man and knew it. The idea of no celebratory photo of me aloft the plinth at John O'Groats was unthinkable so at a cost of an extra £15.00, I held my hands up in surrender – my crude and dishonest negotiations were at a close. I agreed to return in an hour.

Conveniently, next door to Jessops was McCallum's Bar.

Ah yes, McCallum's Bar.

I will remember that particular watering hole for the rest of my life, for it's impossible to dislodge it from my mind – and believe me I've tried.

It was almost two o'clock when I entered the bar, clad in my hi-viz jacket, cycling shorts and shoes, carrying my helmet and panniers. No one batted an eyelid.

In the bar were less than a dozen patrons. Two were fat girls seated at the bar on high stools, alongside them another woman who I took to be the matriarch of the establishment. On the corner of the L-shaped bar were a couple who looked to be in their sixties, but probably weren't – the man, a Charles Hawtrey-cum-Kenneth Williams look-a-like wearing a shirt, waistcoat, and trousers, the latter clearly having had a disagreement with his ankles, as they were halfway up his puny calves. His shoes were a long time away from a Stead and Simpson's window too. He wore National Health glasses, had thinning black hair (greased, naturally), with some strands standing perpendicular to his head.

Standing next to him was a woman in a long, dark coat and old-fashioned 'flower pot' hat, but more about her later.

Perched on the banquet seating along the wall was a man of indiscriminate years, without doubt, not on his first pint of Tenants, nodding his head and tapping his knuckles on the table to music he could hear. Only there wasn't any music.

There were other members of this motley crew loitering but they are mere 'extras' in the cast and the story I am about to tell.

Presiding over this scene was an 18 st barman, no more than 35 years of age, wearing a T-shirt more suitable for a person weighing closer to 10st. His denim jeans seemed to have a great urge to lie closer to terra firma, the end result being three inches of 'builders bum' being displayed whenever he turned round. He had no speaking part, serving drinks and drying glasses his only role. I got the impression he had been there some years and had caught the 'show' that I was about to see many times before.

Impossible as it may seem, I melted into the background, nursing my pint of Stella. Being the coward that I am, I also kept my eyes firmly on the decrepit carpet that had a texture more in keeping with a recently tarmacked road on a very hot day than a deeply piled piece of shag flooring. It was well trodden.

The first 'act' involved a number of 'the cast' retiring to the pavement at regular intervals to share a roll up, while the ageing drummer boy kept up a solo beat to his silent music. Honestly, he would have put Phil Collins to shame with his movement. I was so impressed that I actually found myself offering accompaniment, humming the William Tell Overture as he maintained his steady beat. For those not gifted in the classical music department but are of a certain age, substitute the theme music from *'The Lone Ranger'* TV Western and you will get the picture.

The second 'act' was mime; a mature woman entering the bar clearly promoting the fact that she knew it was 'dress down Wednesday'. She purchased half a pint of strong lager and set about the one-armed bandit with gusto. Alas, her coins were soon gone and she returned to the bar to change more notes – in fact four times she returned to the bar to change more notes.

Working on the basis that even if they were only £5 notes that she changed she was now over £20.00 down. Eventually her luck was at an end, or more to the point her money was at an end. After unsuccessfully rummaging through her bag for more cash she scuttled out, the confused look on her face confirming to me that she genuinely felt that she should have scooped the jackpot.

Perhaps it would be tomorrow when she would metaphorically break the bank at Monte Carlo. One thing was certain – she would be back, subject to bank or social security approval, to exact revenge on that light-flashing glutton of a machine that had devoured that week's housekeeping money in less than 15 minutes.

Do you remember I briefly mentioned the woman standing next to Hawtrey-Williams lookalike? Yes, the one in the long coat and the flower pot hat.

Well, she had been consuming vodka at a truly alarming rate – either that or the barman had been plying her with glasses of Highland Spring water at spirit level prices. My leaning was more towards the former.

Well, she topped the bill – she had an act to die for.

She was an interesting case and even more interesting as the Smirnoff took effect. Similar to a slow moving metronome she would alternate between raucous laughter and aggressive threats, a kind of 'see you Jimmy' one minute and a smile the next. There was nothing in between. The best description I can come up with is that she had four or five mood swings – every minute.

It is my considered view that she was frightening – not to be messed with, so I espied her discreetly.

After a few more 'looseners' of the clear liquid, no doubt to ease her stage fright she decided that she wanted some music on so wandered off to the corner of the room where she spent at least 10 minutes studying the list of tunes available. After the matriarch's intervention due to her being clueless on how a juke box worked, she fed the machine with coins, made her selection, then rejoined her friends. Her choice was made and the music came on.

Suddenly, she burst into life, shouting: 'Och this is my wee favourite' in a surprised tone, all the more surprising to me as only 30 seconds earlier she had selected that bloody record. Warming to her cabaret task, she then placed one hand behind her back, the other above her head and started to revolve in rapidly increasing circles while singing (I use the term loosely) along to the tune. It was a geriatric, drunken 21st century highland jig danced to a 1970 Elvis track.

This set the Hawtrey-Williams man off into shrieks of high-pitched screams – he was clearly an Elvis fan too, or he was when Presley's 'I can't help believing' was played.

As for the barman, he continued to dry his glasses while staring into the middle distance – it could have been an empty bar on a wet Monday in January for all he was concerned. He was getting more enjoyment breathing heavily on the insides of glasses before giving them a final cursory wipe.

From memory, she jigged to three of Presley's greatest hits before finishing her performance with some more of her mood swings. Her curtain call was a rather loud, albeit slurred and, if I may say, uncalled for: 'And you can fuck off John' to her greasy-haired friend, before placing both her elbows on the bar and staring straight ahead into the crack of the barman's arse.

The bar was again silent except for Phil the drummer boy – his beat

159

rolled on.

It was a wonderful 50 minutes that I spent in McCallum's Bar and I was sorry to leave, my instincts telling me that there was still more entertainment to come from the unorthodox cabaret artists.

I may return one day to revisit old friends and acquaintances, if only to catch the late show and see whether their performances changed – when they were really full of liquor.

I re-entered Jessops for my camera and charger at precisely 2.43 p.m. (God only knows why I made a note of the time) and with photographic equipment fully charged and my pocket £30.00 lighter I headed for the Kessock Bridge, a cabled-stayed bridge that carries the main A9 over the inlet of water that separates the Beauly Firth from the Moray.

Lying in the lee of the high bridge is the home of Inverness Caledonian Thistle football club, so the inevitable tour of its stadium's circumference was necessary before attempting the bridge crossing.

The volume of traffic on the bridge was quite astonishing and, together with the strong easterly wind blowing, made progress less than smooth. Dodging glass fragments and sharp gravel was the least of my difficulties as half of Scotland it seemed had some terribly important matters to attend to on the north coast.

I found myself saying a quiet prayer of thanks that the laughing cavaliers in McCallum's Bar had no access to a car but kept a vigilant eye and ear cocked just in case I was wrong. Never mind Elvis's 'I'm a believer' being my favourite, more in my mind was: 'I'm a Survivor'.

In many ways I was sorry that I couldn't stay longer in Inverness. I had first visited the place before in my travel days, but it had grown considerably since then; its current population of 60,000 being 50 per cent more than only 20 years ago.

Charles Kennedy, the former leader of the Liberal Democrats was born in this thrusting and thriving city and was probably no stranger to McCallum's Bar – so too was Derry Irvine the former Lord Chancellor under Tony Blair.

It's renowned for its high quality of life and judging by some of the residents I encountered its high quantity of life too.

After the Kessock Bridge, the trunk road continued on a dual carriageway up along a hard climb for five or six miles, then descended again to cross the next stretch of water spearing inland, the Cromarty Firth.

This bridge, which on first sight looked slightly thinner than the Great Yarmouth pier was even more dangerous than Kessock. While this one crossed the Firth at ground level it did not possess a cycle lane, so the same volume of lorries, vans, cars and motor bikes buffeted me at a rate of a vehicle every three seconds. My only consolation was that I was just 109 miles from John O'Groats.

Fortunately the nightmare crossing was soon behind me, and I was able to reassure my bowels that they would not be called upon to perform any further functions until 8.00-8.30 the next morning. I think we were both relieved. It's an interesting thought that – a cure for all people afflicted with constipation – one, maximum two, bike rides over the Cromarty bridge and one would be regular for life.

More through luck than judgement I safely crossed my second expanse of water and headed north-east along the shoreline of the Cromarty Firth to the Novar Arms at Evanton.

Evanton is a village that overlooks the Firth, that's if you are brave enough to venture out to look. I remembered telephoning the hotel a few times when arranging accommodation (computers still being instruments for sissies up here) and was never able to make myself heard over the din from the bar. It crossed my mind that the Novar Arms and McCallum's Bar may have a reciprocal arrangement – swapping customers, so each can enjoy a city break or coastal holiday without leaving a bar.

A good friend of mine who came from these parts told me that he was too frightened to drive through Evanton in the late 60s on his way from Tain to Dingwall – and he was a nightclub bouncer. Since then he said it had gone down hill badly. And there was me, wondering for the last 40 years why he had moved to Christchurch, New Zealand.

Of course, I assumed he was exaggerating, but changed my mind after 'Googling' Evanton for some background information. The reply came back: 'Who wants to know?'

I checked in and was given a room on the third floor at the back of the hotel. In addition I was given a key for a ground floor room with the tip to lock my bike up in there and lock the door. I was also told if I liked that room better I could sleep with my bike – it was that kind of hotel.

Studying the menu in the bar that evening I cracked; my confidence had gone completely – all the warnings about the place had taken their toll. I decided that to avoid a possible ruck, the best course of action would be for me to ask the waitress what she would like to recommend for dinner instead of me causing trouble by choosing.

I concluded my crawling by telling her that she could bring it in her own good time whenever she had a moment. I even offered to pay her up front. You see, I have the spine of a jellyfish when it comes to violence, and it is never long before it bubbles to the surface.

Needless to say I congratulated the waitress on the quality of food and her excellent service but felt rather foolish when she told me that she hadn't brought it yet.

Yes, I know, I'm a coward and panicked – but I got out alive.

Trust me, the Novar Arms in Evanton is not for the squeamish as I was to have confirmed many months later. A newspaper article I read told how two policemen were held hostage in the pub by a drunken customer who had taken a dislike to the landlord who wanted to close up for the night.

The Novar Arms: not for the faint hearted.

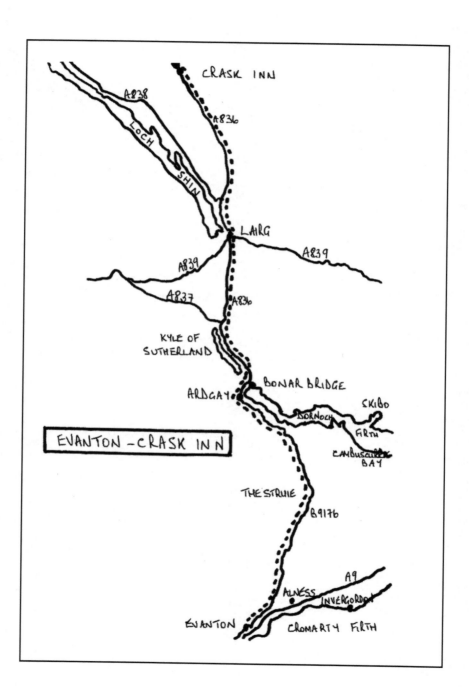

Day 14
Evanton to the Crask Inn

IN the middle of the night I was awoken by the shrill of the hotel telephone. It was the early hours of the morning and my dull, sleep-addled brain fought valiantly to kick-start itself into life.

Who was calling at this ridiculous hour?

Was I was being called down to the bar as a reinforcement in a fight? Had my bike been stolen and being offered back to me at a special rate? Was there a family problem? Isn't it amazing how quickly questions flash through the mind when some silly bugger telephones out of hours.

Fortunately it was none of the above, only my old friend, Iain Marshall calling from New Zealand. Marshy was my biggest sponsor and was no doubt calling to check that his money was being spent wisely. Even though he had lived in the Antipodes for 40 years he had not lost a single syllable of his broad Scottish accent, having originated from the small village of Inver not more than 20 miles from where I was lying.

He wanted to know how my ride was going and I was pleased to tell him that overall things were fine except for the odd lumpy bits that his country had thrown at me two days earlier. He asked me my route to John O'Groats and I told him that I was heading due north over the Struie to Ardgay, Bonar Bridge, and Lairg, then across the wilds to the north coast.

'Don't go over the Struie,' he shouted from 13,000 miles away, 'It will kill you – ride up the A9 to Tain.'

An expletive flashed in seconds across the world as I impolitely informed him I would not travel up the A9 in an Army tank, let alone a push-bike, following my experiences of the traffic on the bridges coming out of Inverness. We eventually closed our conversation with Marshy having the last word: 'Don't say I didn't warn you'.

I was still raw from the Lecht, so the warning that the Struie would get me meant that the remainder of the night passed uncomfortably. Two days ago I had never heard of the Lecht – now it was the Struie.

On another cold, grey day I left Evanton a shade before 09.00 a.m. and, just prior to entering Alness, took the B9176 north. It was good cycling weather and I knew that Bonar Bridge was only 23 miles away but with the Struie in between. Whether the Struie constituted all 23 of those miles or just one I did not know. What I did know was that the Struie and I were about to meet and an old friend had warned me of its power.

Fortunately this time it was good news; the warning, unlike Spock's two day's previous, was totally unfounded.

Forty years in Australia and New Zealand had definitely clouded my friend's mind and memory of the Struie – it came and went without it even troubling my lowest gear. I would like to say I was getting stronger, fitter, more mentally disciplined, but I would be lying – the Struie was a pussycat and it rolled over and let me tickle its tummy.

I can only assume that my good friend, Iain Marshall rode over the Struie on his tricycle when he was about four years of age. And knowing Marshall as I do, in the middle of winter.

I felt good as I rode up to the summit and looked east over Dornoch Firth and into the beautifully shaped cove which shelters Skibo Castle, the venue for Madonna and Guy Ritchie's wedding. Although it was overcast and not conducive for photographs the view was still stunning; the long road bridge over the Firth making a jaw-dropping backdrop to Cambuscurrie Bay.

I freewheeled down into Ardgay and across the bottom of Kyle of

Sutherland water into Bonar Bridge, and, by a vote of one to zero, decided to stop for a cup of coffee.

Mentally and physically I felt fine, even though bouts of loneliness were never far from the surface. I rationalised that I had handled the solo ride so far by doing my percentages of 'distance ridden versus distance to go' and could quite happily do that for a few more days. The mental arithmetic, regular drinks, sightseeing, and many hours of 'brain in neutral' were seeing me through quite nicely. I was also relatively sure that the worst bits were behind me and my last few days would be trouble free.

I was into a rhythm and while on occasions it was monotonous, I was making great progress. Physically, I was in good shape for a man of my age on his first long ride of his life. A slightly sore arse at the end of each day, yes, but no open sores – other than the ones inflicted in the accident in Cornwall.

In short, I could almost see the finishing line and was feeling mighty proud of myself.

Bonar Bridge is a truly beautiful village, right on the border of Sutherland and Ross and Cromarty. With a population of about 1,000 it is similar to the size of Chadlington, my village in the Cotswolds; large enough not to know everyone's business by natural gossip, but small enough to, if you really tried.

I drank my coffee in a coffee shop that also sold souvenirs and nick-nacks, and got into conversation with an English couple that lived in Ardgay, the village two miles south, right at the head of the Dornoch Firth.

Jim and his wife loved their home and also loved walking, and he told me that their next break would be walking in the Cotswolds, as they particularly wanted to walk in the area of Cleeve Hill.

My first thought was that he was teasing me. My surname is Cleevely and my name originates from me being born under the lee of Cleeve Hill , just outside Cheltenham. It's a small old world isn't it? Me in the frozen wastes of Sutherland talking to an English couple who want to walk across a part of the Cotswolds that bears my name.

Like a lot of people I met on my ride, Jim was a class act and had no hesitation in giving me £5.00 for the charity I was riding for. If you ever read this Jim, many thanks, the 20 minutes I spent chatting with you and your wife were very welcome.

Soon I was back in the saddle and pushing on up the A836 to Inveran and Lairg. The terrain was now very easy with no major climbs, just little inclines to test the legs and downhill sections to relax. This far north the A roads are a bit of a joke – they are not A roads at all, merely like tiny English country lanes about 10 ft wide, but with less traffic.

On route to Lairg I stopped by the Falls of Shin, a place I hadn't visited since touring Scotland by car with my wife, way back in 1974. Then the Falls were secluded and a natural attraction, but now they had cultivated paths, handrails, and viewing platforms – natural beauty replaced by artificial surroundings pleasing only to a Health and Safety jobsworth.

Sure the River Shin still cascaded down over unspoiled rocks and boulders, and salmon leap as they head upstream to spawn, but if Al Fayed, the owner could make a few more bob reversing the flow of the river, I am sure he would try.

Why, there is even a small Harrods-style restaurant and gift shop peddling souvenirs – more reasons to relieve you of your small change and high denomination notes. Since my last visit, the Falls had altered from a natural, unspoiled beauty spot in the Highlands of Scotland to a Knightsbridge cashpoint with a waterfall.

Is that improvement or commercial vandalism?

Salmon leaping reminded me of one of my favourite stories. Two salmon were battling upstream to spawn and were only halfway up and totally and utterly exhausted. As they were regaining strength in a rock pool one said to the other: 'Sod this for a game of soldiers, I'm knackered. Why don't we just stop here and have a wank?'

Apocryphal – definitely. Poor taste – certainly. Crude – absolutely.

Amusing though, none the less.

I took the lane out of the Falls of Shin that runs parallel with the A836 but in honesty it was hard to tell the difference. One had no traffic on it at all and the other one was empty.

In Lairg I stopped outside a Spar store to ask directions to the Crask Inn. So far north on single lane roads, one wrong move can take an unsuspecting traveller many miles off course and I wanted to be certain that the solitary road I was taking was not heading for the west coast but north to my overnight destination.

What is it about asking directions from locals that changes them from normal people into gibbering idiots? Or is it my fault, for asking the wrong people.

From the start of my marathon ride I had received wayward information from morons living as far apart as Stibb Cross, the Forest of Dean, Ross on Wye, and the Forth Road Bridge, and I could not recall asking anyone for directions who actually understood my question, never mind the ability to provide me with a lucid answer.

The woman who came out of the Spar shop didn't disappoint. I feared the worst when she started to suck in her breath through clenched teeth while, at the same time, alternating her gaze between me, my bike and into the middle distance across the Firth. I had already anticipated her reaction to my question would be exactly the same reaction to that shown by everyone I had asked since I left Land's End. Bless her, she was perfectly trained.

All I said was: 'Is this the road to the Crask Inn?'

Pointing first one way then the other, it was an immediate dead giveaway – she was clueless. Her hands dropped to her hips, a classic frown appeared on her brow, she even looked to the sky for divine intervention. Completely and utterly stark raving mad – she probably had trouble finding her way home.

Luckily an Englishman who had lived in these parts for many years came over just as she was giving me a very lifelike impression of a Dutch windmill, waving her arms in all directions while saying: 'No, I lie, turn left at the end of the road, no right, hang on a minute, no it's left, or is it. Just a second, I know this one. By car it's about an hour.'

And so it went on.

The man kindly let her down lightly explaining to her that he knew The Crask well. He would deal with my query.

The last we saw of her was walking up the road still waving her arms this way and that, spasmodically turning round to gesture that I should follow her.

On reflection I would put her down as one of the favourites to win the next Lairg 'getting lost in a phone box' championships. She was good fun, but totally useless, except to bring belated smiles to my face long after I had departed from the Spar shop in Lairg.

As it happened the directions to the Crask Inn were very simple. Keep the sun behind, pedal up the A836 and stop at the first white building you come to – about 15 miles up the road.

They were simple and easy directions. Surprisingly, the lady I had approached was unerringly accurate about the time it would take, even though her estimate was for a car not a bike.

Let's just say she was work in progress.

It was now a fabulous day; no breeze, sun shining and blue sky above. I set off along the single-track road - the wild moorland on all sides, mountains in the distance.

The poles to assist snowploughs were back and small lay-bys were cut every 200 yards, in case two cars happened to be within 50 miles of one another and wished to pass. Peat squares had been cut and were laid out to dry, and acres of pine trees were felled and waiting to be collected. They would be taken to Sweden for paper manufacture or mulched and re-glued for cheap wood panels.

I can't say it was a pretty landscape, more of a natural beauty with moors, forests, rocky rivers and streams, yellow gorse and grassland all surrounded by the mighty imposing hills of Sutherland. In a month's time, it would be pretty though, a sea of purple heather covering much of the moor.

Sadly, I would be long gone.

The 15 mile ride up past Loch Beannach to the Crask Inn was quite magical. No cars and perhaps a dozen cottages was all that dotted the landscape. It was just me with nature.

Sure, for much of the year the road is impassable, but on the right day with the right weather it takes some beating. In fact for peace, serenity, solitude and wild beauty it cannot be beaten. I would defy anyone to be stressed cycling in this paradise on a warm summer's day.

Just as I thought I was heading up the wrong lonely road and my next village would be Laxford Bridge on the west coast I saw a white building in the distance. I rode closer. Could it be the famous Crask Inn that I had been told so much about?

It was and I could close another chapter of my ride. I had reached my destination.

It's hard to do justice to the 19th century Crask Inn that Mike and Kai Geldred run – words aren't able to transmit the simple warmth and welcome that is shown to every guest. The Inn is reputed to be the remotest pub in Britain. It has no TV, no computer and the electricity comes from a generator. Its evening meals are most definitely table d'hôte not à la carte.

But when the views of the magnificent Scottish countryside are added to a few beers and the company of people drawn from all walks of life, the conversation just flows. For urban dwellers it's a haven; a good, old-fashioned Inn where the troubles of life just melt away.

I was so lucky. For fully an hour before dinner I was treated to a selection of Scottish reels and folk songs all played on the accordion by a guest who regularly travelled up from Edinburgh to help Mike with his 50 lambing ewes and 20 cattle. Can you imagine sitting in the remotest pub in Britain, looking out over a magical landscape, pint in hand, listening to wistful ditties played on the accordion? Absolutely priceless.

If you're ever passing the Crask Inn, which I doubt, call in – if you're not, make a detour.

It is truly a different world.

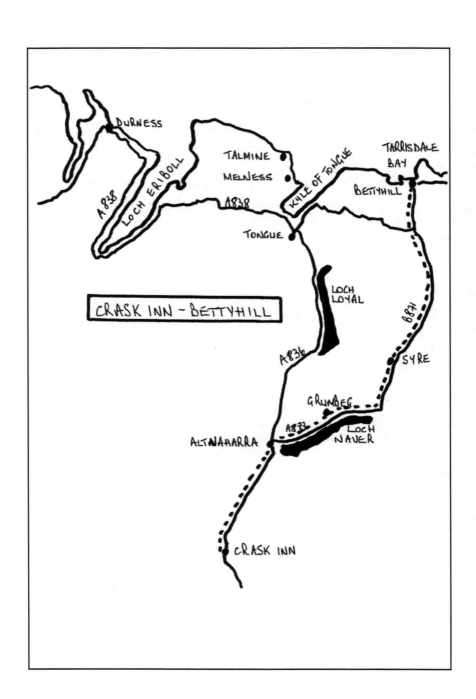

Day 15
The Crask Inn to Bettyhill

STAYING at the Crask Inn not only added a further day to my ride, it also added a day to my stay in Wick after my ride had been completed. An extra two days in total – and I don't regret them for a second.

Let me explain.

From Evanton to Bettyhill, without stopping at The Crask Inn, was 79 easy-riding miles which I could have coped with comfortably in a day. From there it was a further 68 miles to John O'Groats and on down to Wick. If I had followed that schedule I would have been able to catch the early train on Saturday morning for the 13-hour journey back home.

However, by delaying my stay by a day at the Crask Inn, the one and only train out of Wick on a Sunday would have taken a grand total of 23 hours to get me back to my home in the Cotswolds, so I decided to stay an extra day and catch the faster train on Monday.

Can you believe that it takes more time to travel from Wick to Chadlington than it does from Chadlington to Perth, in Australia? Come back British Rail I say – all is forgiven.

In honesty the benefits were many. A slower, more leisurely cycle ride as I neared John O'Groats, a night at the Crask Inn, and a relaxing day in Wick to reflect on my adventure. Oh, and an opportunity to visit Wetherspoons in Wick to slake a raging thirst that had been slowly building up for a fortnight. More of Wetherspoons later.

So, two days added to my 'End-to-End' ride all because of the Crask Inn. Praise indeed for Mike and Kai's hospitality. Needless to say, I hadn't been disappointed.

With a pathetic 33 miles being my challenge for the day I lingered over breakfast and took the opportunity to explore the surroundings where Kai and Mike lived all year round.

The land was covered in white hare's-tail cotton grass and just waiting for the heather to flower. In less than a month it would be an endless sea of purple. Even now it was a sight to behold.

I sat out in the early morning sun talking to Willie, an ex-merchant seaman who used to work at the Rolls-Royce nuclear plant in Thurso. Now retired, he is a volunteer who oversees the Duke of Edinburgh Award Scheme as well as being a member of a Scottish mountain rescue team.

I thought I had enjoyed a pretty rounded life until I heard some of Willie's stories. I was wrong. He told me about his job at the nuclear plant, he even made his nose glow as a finale, before moving on to tell me a little about the volunteer work he so much enjoyed.

Today's Duke of Edinburgh Award hopefuls were from Heriot's School in Edinburgh and were due to pass by the inn mid-morning. I hoped none of them would want a shower as an hour earlier the generator had been playing silly buggers, my shower and a shave being cancelled due to unfavourable generator conditions. Whether the generator could be kick-started into life by the time any new guests arrived was in the lap of the gods.

As with all the regular guests it wasn't long before Willie got round to talking about his happy days at the inn especially the bird life he had seen in the area during his frequent visits.

Eagles, ospreys, siskins, swallows, house martins, chaffinches and starlings were all regular visitors on the long drawn-out days of summer, a sheer paradise for budding ornithologists. I admitted to Willie that I loved bird watching, especially when they were feeding their young, but hadn't done much since my third court appearance for voyeurism.

Kai joined us and was soon making me smile with her infectious, cackling laugh. Both Mike and Kai are Christian folk who see the good in everyone and rarely spot bad – a total contrast to me. They both take whatever life and the weather throws at them and thank the Lord for it. It flashed through my mind I could have learned so much from them if I had started about 50 years earlier.

Just before I left, a Dutch cyclist came through and asked Kai if she would fill his water bottle. She did so happily. When it was returned he looked at the contents and saw a light brown liquid. It reminded me of the water in Spanish Hotels in the 1970s. I didn't drink it then and I doubt if the Dutchman drank it now. He left with a bemused smile, while Kai wished him a safe and speedy journey. The word healthy was never mentioned.

I eventually dragged myself away from Mike and Kai's home at 11.00 a.m., still bewitched by the slow way of life and completely enraptured by the simple things that satisfied my hosts. Up here in the natural wilds of Sutherland they lead an uncomplicated life, ignoring Wi-Fi, emails, TVs, Facebook and Twitter, and all the other electronic paraphernalia that clogs minds. They just go through life simply, accepting the weather and its accompanying hardships as an act of God. Not my cup of tea all day, every day, but you have to admire their stoicism.

Again the weather was ideal for cycling as I headed off up the busy A836 – well quite busy anyway, a car passing the inn little more than two hours earlier.

Wild country was all around me as I rode due north on the flat, well maintained road, the magnificent peaks of the Meall an Fhuarain and 3,000 ft Meall nan Con munros looming high either side of me. It was easy riding – it was peaceful and the surroundings beautiful.

Soon I was in Altnaharra at the foot of Loch Naver, a small settlement of less than 20 houses and farms. Along with Braemar it vies for the right to be described as the coldest place in Great Britain, Altnaharra's claim to fame being backed by a chilly -29°C in 1995. Today though it was cool, bordering on cold, but to the hardy souls of this Sutherland outpost it probably felt a touch humid.

At Altnaharra I turned eastwards off the A836 that continued on to Tongue, to head along the north bank of Loch Naver, along a track euphemistically called the B873.

Following the bank but about 100 ft up, the track provided me with even more staggering views across the loch to Loch Choire Forest. As well as the tranquil beauty, I couldn't believe that this part of Sutherland provided me with so much flat riding – I was expecting a continuation of my Grampian trials and tribulations.

Midway along the loch I chanced upon the most interesting historic landmark of my whole ride – in my view emulating St Michael's Mount, Tintagel, Tintern Abbey, Ironbridge – even the fast food shops of Leigh.

I arrived at Grumbeg, or to be precise where Grumbeg had once been.

You see, Grumbeg was caught up in one of the first recorded cases of ethnic cleansing in history. Sadly, their few stone cottages were similar to the many settlements that were dotted around the Sutherland region in the early 19th century. At that time there were thousands of simple crofters eking a living off the land as best they could by shepherding their small herds of sheep and cows as well as growing any basic food the barren land would allow. They were no trouble to anyone and were just about surviving in conditions that were frugal and harsh.

Then came what history calls the Highland Clearances.

In 1814, the Lairds of the Countess of Sutherland's 1.5 million acre estate decreed that everyone who lived there should be moved to enable shepherds from the border country in the south to lease the land for their sheep at a much higher rent. All told 15,000 crofters were forcibly removed, cottages and whole villages razed to the ground as people were pushed to the coast and islands. It led to the first wave of Britons moving overseas with mass emigration to the North America colonies.

Everyone who had lived there peacefully, remember ancestors had for centuries, was literally swept away, never to return.

The ruins of Grumbeg still remain, a poignant reminder to those days almost 200 years ago when a population the size of a small town was shooed off the land and ordered to find an alternative home – even if it was 4,000 miles away. The Lairds of Sutherland you see weren't interested in fairness, merely how to extract a few extra sovereigns from their tenants. Their greed and avarice came way up their list before human kindness and morals.

Grumbeg: a deserted but touchingly emotional reminder of man's cruelty to man.

As I clambered back to the road after examining the Gumberg ruins, a small group of cyclists rode by. There were about six of them, along with an escort car. We exchanged nods of respect, rather like two boxers touching gloves as they came out for their final round. I was quietly confident that they would have given me two nods if they had known that my journey had commenced at Land's End.

At the end of the loch I turned north again and tracked the River Naver through the village of Syre – village being a touch kind, as it only contained six houses. From there the river flows only a few yards from the road for the 10 miles to Bettyhill before disgorging its contents into the North Sea at Torrisdale Bay.

So far since leaving the Crask the day had been kind to me. I had enjoyed splendid scenery, good road conditions and ideal weather. If you will excuse the pun, the day had been a breeze. But as I neared the coast a strong northerly wind sprung up, at stages reducing me to almost walking pace.

It had become really tough going with the strongest wind I had experienced on my whole ride. Even if it was a short day the elements were not letting me cruise to my destination, they were still testing my resolve.

The last 10 miles of the day proved to be hard work but not stressful psychologically – with less than 60 miles to the 'end of the line' it was not difficult to smile as I laboured up the hills knowing that I was counting each one down to the finish.

Just outside Bettyhill I met up with the A836 again, the road that I had first joined way south of Bonar Bridge. At Altnaharra it had continued north to Tongue but now it had angled back east to take me all the way to John O'Groats.

Suddenly, coming over a brow in the road I saw the North Sea for the first time and what a sight it was. There before me was the mouth of the River Naver slowly flowing into the sea over the widest sandy beach you could possibly imagine.

With the sun shining it was an unbelievably panoramic view. Just two weeks earlier I had been gazing out over the Atlantic in identical weather conditions, now I was gazing again but this time over a stretch of unspoiled sand 1,000 road miles further north.

No injection could have stimulated more adrenalin than that which flowed through my veins at that moment. Looking west, then east along the shoreline I knew I was oh-so-close to the end of my epic solo trip.

I was soon at my hotel, a one-star establishment masquerading as two, and quickly found my way to the bar for an end of day drink. It was a shade before two.

In the bar, lunching, were the six cyclists I had seen earlier. They recognised me instantly and asked me how far I had come. The conversation went something like this.

'Have you ridden far?'

'Yeah, up from Land's End.'

'Bloody hell lads, did you hear that, he's ridden up from Land's End.

Congratulations, that's an amazing feat.'

'Thanks, I suppose it's not bad.'

'Not bad? Absolutely brilliant – you've ridden solo from Land's End.' How long did it take you?"

'A fortnight. What are you lads doing, just a bit of touring in the area?'

'No, we've come up from Land's End too – in 10 days.'

End of conversation.

Regardless of the fact that they were 40 years younger than me, had a back up support vehicle carrying their baggage, and had taken a more direct route than me I felt the poor relation: a crumpled old man compared to the six sleek, tanned, frightfully fit fanatics, that had stopped by for lunch before breezing on to John O'Groats later that afternoon.

It was a classic case of hero to zero in five seconds.

I retired to my room to dry my cycling gear. I would also have had a bath there too but it would have meant physical exertions getting in and out of the washbasin, the hotel not having the time, money or possibly the inclination to bring their establishment into the 21st century.

In all the B&Bs I had stayed in so far the bathroom was usually next door to my room, or at the very worst across the corridor. The Bettyhill hotel didn't work quite like that. Sod's law decreed that there were two bathrooms on my floor, exactly equidistant from my room, but both a short taxi ride away.

To say they were both in need of modernisation would be the same as suggesting that Tiger Woods had requested relief for his balls when they were lodged in a bit of rough – it was that obvious.

My guess is that Armitage Shanks's great-great-grandfather had been but a twinkle in his mother's eye when this line of basic bathroom porcelain was installed.

I'd go even further and say that bidets were still a fussy addition only used by Johnny Foreigner across the Channel. And then only to clean the mud off their dirty football boots after a game against some Italian poofters in Nancy.

And I'll tell you another thing - its not often you see a toilet chain, minus the wooden handle loitering without intent in a hotel bathroom these days. Put it this way, if it had worked efficiently 17 people in the bar would have been spared the news that one of its residents had just had an almighty dump and had been unable to dispense with it. My guess is that the noise abatement society, or the local water board come to that, would position that toilet well above the natural miracles of Niagara or Iguassu Falls on both thunderous din and volume.

Both the washbasin and bath had further evidence that they were installed about the same time as the Highland Clearances; constantly dripping taps already forming stalagmites close to the plugholes. Unsuspecting clientèle could have lost an eye.

But even antiquated bathrooms have benefits. After bathing in the deepest bath I have ever seen, I suspected that I would have trouble getting out, so steep were the sides. As luck would have it many patrons before me had made my life easier, the tidemark ringing the bath being a handy foothold to set me free – a bit crusty certainly but useful in the extreme.

Many of you who have frequented this type of hotel – and to be fair the £25.00 charged for bed and breakfast represented good value for money – will know what is coming next.

I was faced with the eternal conundrum, one that I have never been able to resolve.

Do I put my old gear back on or risk a towel hastily knotted round the waist?

It's always the towel, isn't it? And it's always the wrong choice.

I say that for two reasons.

The first is that cheap hotels always provide you with towels slightly smaller than the size of an average face flannel – giving the male guest the choice of either covering his wedding tackle or his arse – but never both.

The other strange quirk is that however quiet the hotel is, it is guaranteed that at the precise moment that you decide to head back to the comfort and safety of your own quarters, another guest, usually female, will be walking towards you along the corridor.

Not a problem you may say, but remember this. After you have passed, I promise you they will always, yes, always, look back and see your hairy behind smiling at them with a couple of your ripe plums doing the cha-cha-cha just below.

To make matters worse that same person is guaranteed to be sitting at the next table to you in the bar that evening, with both of you knowing that her smirks and giggles are the result of her now being aware that you are an untidy housekeeper in the business area.

Now deep into old age it is virtually impossible for me to have any credibility with any females under the age of at least 50 – and then only if they are desperate and full of Bacardi. Oh for the days when I was known as the King of chat.

Do you know, I had a plan when chatting woman up that never ever failed me.

All it took was: 'Excuse me miss, does this damp cloth smell of chloroform to you?'

Happy days.

The World Cup had started in South Africa so the boredom of my own company was relieved as I ate dinner, even if it was a totally forgettable fixture between Uruguay and France.

It would be wrong of me to say that the bar in the Bettyhill hotel acted like a magnet for the social elite of the north coast, so well in advance of the game ending I was back in my room thinking ahead to my final day on the road. I was also wondering whether my voyeuristic friend would knock on my door to ask if her female companion could give me a second opinion on my personal possessions.

Alas, sleep came quickly that night.

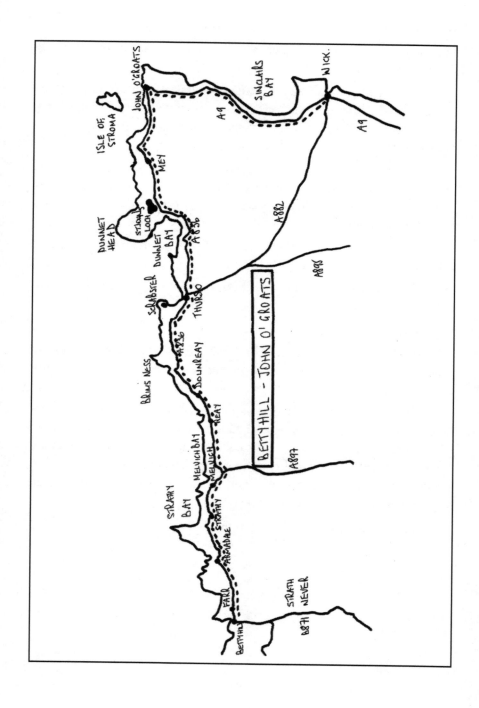

Day 16
Bettyhill to John O'Groats

WOW! This was the day I had never got around to thinking about: the last day of my ride. just 51 more miles, along the north coast of Scotland, and I would be at John O'Groats, my destination.

Due to my early night and probably because of an adrenalin surge, I was up prompt at seven, showered and packed by 7.20 a.m. and waiting for the breakfast room to open 10 minutes later. I wanted to eat and get on the road early but my plans did not synchronise particularly well with the breakfast servers. There was only one winner, them, and it was past 8.30 a.m. when I eventually hit the road.

The first 10 miles was like the Blackpool big dipper (with only the dried sick and smell of pee missing), the road dropping steeply in and out of Farr and Armadale Bays on its way to Strathy. The wind was also causing problems, first from the side then head on, and with wind and steep pulls out of coves testing my resolve it was clear that my 'End-to-End' adventure was finishing with a sting in its tail.

Once past Strathy, the road headed inland a mile or so, away from the bays, and sufficient to take the lumps out of the road. I began to make good time.

Between Melvich and Reay a slow trickle of cyclists began to approach me, I assumed attempting the 'End-to-End' from north to south.

In the tradition of a good touring cyclist I nodded and bid them a hearty good morning. The first few totally ignored me and pressed on, but slower ones were more than happy to return my greeting by way of a curt nod. After my fiftieth nod and smile, I felt a bit like 'Churchill', that loathsome bloody insurance dog seen nodding away on TV commercials.

Oh, and one more thing, and I can be quite categorical here – if one more cyclist had shouted to me: 'You're going the wrong way' I would have dragged them off their bike, shoved a pump up them and asked: 'Would 32 lb pressure per square inch suit you sir?'

It turned out that none of the 500-plus cyclists were heading for Land's End at all, they were all competitors in an 84-mile race round the north coast. If I told you that in the first 12 miles of the race the distance between the first and last cyclist was 11 miles you will understand the difference in class.

Besides the cyclists making my final day interesting, I was also fascinated by what was left of the Dounreay Nuclear Power Development Establishment. To say it is a wee blot on the stunning coastal landscape is like suggesting eating 20,000 calories a day and taking no exercise may possibly cause obesity – its blindingly bloody obvious. The Dounreay nuclear power station is an absolute monstrosity.

It was initially built in 1955 by the Government to develop fast breeder reactor technology using uranium as a nuclear fuel. But get this: it took until June 1998, a cool 43 years, for some bright spark (quite literally) to state that there may be some safety issues to consider. Why nobody noticed that local residents had been walking round for two score years and three with their heads flashing like a Belisha beacon is anybody's guess.

It's now 'tidy up time' at the plant with the overall task scheduled to continue until 2025. Still plenty of time to set up some twin town arrangements with Chernobyl then.

Whether the overall project had been deemed a success, I don't know. What I do know is that the 60 metre giant steel sphere surrounding the first reactor is an ugly testament to the research, and has been for nigh on 55 years.

Conditions were good as I cycled the 10 miles to Thurso, the roads flat and the northerly wind blowing across me. I was now just 30 miles from John O'Groats and able to start my countdown, mile by mile.

I concluded that riding solo from the south-west of England to the north-east of Scotland presents many challenges, some physical, but most mental. Let me explain.

There can be no doubt that Great Britain is a truly beautiful island with ever changing scenery. Whether it be the steep lanes and dainty coves of Cornwall, the wandering River Wye in Monmouthshire, the Bowland Fells in north-east Lancashire, the Border country, or the Scottish Highlands, the attraction they offer can only hold your interest for a certain period of time.

What I am saying is, that in spite of the scenery there are many hours when the ride is just a bloody hard grind. Remember, I was alone.

Physically there are always risks for a cyclist, even more so when they are attempting an 'End-to-End' ride halfway through their seventh decade. Backsides do get sore riding 70 miles plus every day, knee joints twinge, fingers develop pins and needles and necks stiffen. Crashes, or the thought of them, are never far away, plus a whole lot more.

But the real challenge for me was coping with the mental side of each day. After the landscape had been admired, the lambs gambolling enjoyed, the inclines beaten and yet another sight of tumbling water over a rocky bed marvelled at, there were the long hard miles when nothing much was happening except the need to revolve the pedals of the bike.

For mile after mile, turning the pedals became the only source of interest and after the trillionth time even that loses its novelty and gets a bit samey. No company, no outstanding scenery, no blow up doll, nothing, just you and the road ahead seemingly never ending.

It's an identical routine, all day, every day, for two solid weeks. And, at the close of each day when the riding is over, maybe a brief greeting by the B&B host before more silence over a solitary dinner. After that, bed, and another day of the same.

Trust me it takes discipline, especially in bad weather when morale is low and the world seems to be against you. It truly takes discipline.

So to a great degree the physical endurance is secondary, it's the mental strength that is required. Don't get me wrong, I am not complaining, it was my choice to do the ride and do it alone – I am just making the point that it is far more of a mental challenge when riding solo.

I was able to cope by doing my 'percentages': checking and rechecking the distance I had travelled and the distance still to go, converting those two statistics into a percentage of the day's route completed – then estimating a time of arrival on points up the line.

It kept my mind active and alert and went some way to arresting the eternal boredom. Add that arithmetic game to target setting for drinks and snacks and my never waning interest in village names on signposts passed and you will get about five per cent towards understanding what I am trying to say. It's all in the mind.

The end of the dream was only 20 miles distant when I arrived in Thurso, the largest town on the north coast, overlooking the Orkney Islands. It's solid and grey. While many of the inhabitants were still employed running down the Dounreay operation, a thriving white fish industry had been developed in Scrabster, just outside the town.

Besides the fish initiative, the eco-brigade had also arrived. Soon, near the town, 21 wind turbines would be built, capable, allegedly, of powering 25,000 homes. As Thurso only has 3,000, Crask Inn must be in with a shout. Every cloud, eh?

I've got to say that the residents of Thurso have not been dealt the greatest of hands have they? A massively ugly nuclear reactor up the road for 50-odd years, now unsightly windmills on their doorstep, plus the reek of rotting fish.

If I were Thurso born-and-bred I would think that life was a bitch at times. And do you know something? I think I might be right.

Within 20 minutes of leaving Thurso it was decision time. When riding alongside the wide, sandy, crescent shaped beach of Dunnet Bay it crossed my mind to head the three miles due north to visit Dunnet Head, officially the most northerly point on the British mainland. I could see it in the distance rising above the waves and I was tempted.

After thoughts lasting all of 10 seconds I sidestepped the detour, for four solid reasons.

Firstly, as I had not visited the most southerly point on the mainland, that being the Lizard Point in Cornwall, there weren't any bragging rights to be gained by visiting the most northerly one.

Secondly, I had spied plenty of lighthouses on the TV programme 'Coast' and decided that one was much the same as another – an erect phallic symbol, usually painted red and white, with a flashing torch stuck out of the business end.

My third reason was that looking out to sea at Dunnet Head would be just the same as looking out to sea anywhere else – grey water with little white bits flecking the top.

And my final reason was – I was too bloody idle.

The only concession I gave it was a quick photograph when approaching Castlehill.

On I pressed past St John's Loch towards Mey. It was here that I experienced true humiliation – a young girl, not yet out of her teens, overtaking me, dare I say, riding an ancient bike with a chain gagging for a gargle of oil. To rub my nose in it, she slowed when reaching me and we chatted.

She told me that she was employed at Castle Mey, the summer residence of the late Queen Mother, and was in a hurry as she was late for work. She moved ahead and started the long incline up to the Castle entrance, her bike almost identical to ones I had last seen in Enid Blyton's Secret Seven books when I was about nine. People of a certain age will remember the type. It was when having a Sturmey Archer 3-speed was a big deal. Well she had one.

It would be nice to report that a good old bike always beats a good new one , but I cannot lie. She toiled badly on the hill, her 3-speeds being about 12 gears too few, and it was with some reluctance that I rode past her apologetically explaining that I was in a hurry too.

Castle Mey was another popular tourist spot that I declined to visit, primarily because I was only 6 miles from my goal and was keen to get to the finish. Besides, I knew that the star of the show would not have the kettle on for me, the dear old lady having passed away eight years earlier.

I also estimated that she had had 55 opportunities to send me a birthday card and had failed miserably every single year so I owed her nothing. Two can play at that game. Besides I had bigger fish to fry, Castle Mey could wait for another day.

I genuinely can't remember much about the last 30 minutes of my ride from Castle Mey to John O'Groats. The road was flat, the scenery ordinary, and my teenage cyclist's pert bottom not enough to remain long in my memory. I wish I could bring you to a climax by telling you of the extraordinary levels of excitement I was experiencing but I would be lying if I tried – it was brain in neutral time.

Then, up front I saw the sign that told me that John O'Groats was just a quarter of a mile away. Less than 500 yards and I was home.

After 91 hours 43 minutes of solo riding I had travelled 1067 miles from Land's End and I was now at John O'Groats. The time was 12.42 p.m. on Saturday, 12 June 2010.

I was at my journey's end, a journey that had started on Sunday, 1 November 2009 when I first sat on my static training bike and rode for an hour, that being the first time on a bike – albeit stationary – in almost 50 years.

I rode through the car park and down to the famous signpost directing anyone who cared to enquire that Land's End was way down south and the Orkneys somewhere to the north.

Two other 'End-to-Enders' arrived having travelled up the east coast through Dunbeath and Wick. We exchanged cameras and took the ritual photographs astride the famous concrete plinth - some photographs with sunglasses being worn, some without, a shot in the blue cycling jacket, then one in the red cycling jersey.

'Does my hair look all right – are you sure?'

Try and picture the scene. This moment was the culmination of seven months of single-minded training and two weeks of lonely roads.

On reflection though, it is highly unlikely that you can picture the scene, unless you have just ridden nearly 1,100 solo miles carrying 24 lb of weight in panniers.

But if you do meet the criteria above you will know exactly how I felt.

I, like many thousands every year, had achieved a feat that would have been impossible for me eight months earlier. But in that time I had morphed from a near-15 st sexagenarian, comfortably shifting the best part of a bottle of red wine a night while watching Sky Sports, to a 12 st 'mature athlete' who had ridden from the south-west tip of England to the north-east tip of Scotland and raised a few bob for charity.

I would love to say that for the next hour my mind was a bit hazy, lost in a blur of flashing camera bulbs, TV, radio and press interviews.

It would also be exciting to report that I had heard rumours that my name had been put forward for a CBE or OBE, an MBE at the very least.

But I would be lying – it was just the three of us, standing a little self-consciously watching each other sign the official book before saying our 'well done' and 'safe journey home'. I was just another one of thousands who had battled against the elements for a bit of self-satisfaction and personal pride.

I retired to the café for a coffee and muffin and sent a few texts to the friends and relatives that had kindly supported me all the way through the ride. It wasn't a grand message, just 'Job done, finished at 12.42'.

My wife Christine called and asked me how I felt. Do you know? I couldn't give an answer because I couldn't think of one. I didn't feel anything. It was as though I had been given a business assignment and it had come to an end. I had signed it off – literally, job done.

After only 40 minutes at John O'Groats I was back in the saddle for the 17 miles ride south down the east coast to Wick. Mercifully I had a strong following wind and the journey lasted not much more than an hour. It was a lovely, relaxing end to my marathon – no pressure, breeze on my back, manageable climbs and the glow inside of knowing I had completed LEJOG.

Wick soon came into view and it wasn't long before I was standing outside my final bed and breakfast overlooking the quayside. And, just like all the others it was another cracker.

To round off my eighth Scottish night stop I would stay in a house run by another Sassenach, in this case a Geordie Sassenach – June Burns. Amazingly, seven B&Bs had been English and one, in Bettyhill, Mexican – and not a man wearing a kilt in sight.

For my two night stay, June didn't disappoint – a first-class room and private first floor sitting room over looking the quay – all at the extortionate price of £25.00 a night. Scandalous, eh? I think not. It also included a full launder of my dirty gear and about 1,000 laughs. You see, June is a very funny lady with a wicked sense of humour. She also offers fantastic value for money.

I can't repeat many of her stories but what I can tell you is this: the Chief of Police for Wick has now developed a permanent stammer and twitch after June jumped out and frightened him one too many times.

She also swore to me that a Jehovah's Witness once knocked on her door and she invited him in, sat him down and asked what he wanted to talk about.

He replied: 'Buggered if I know, I've never got this far before.'

Go and see June and ask her about the Jehovah's Witness and the shivering policeman, I'm sure she will tell you the stories. But watch out, she is stark raving bonkers, in the most lovely of ways.

June introduced me to the Wetherspoons pub restaurant, a company

I had heard of but never tried, assuming that anyone over 22 years of age was classed as persona non grata.

Well what a pleasant surprise.

Where else can you get three excellent pints of real ale, a large plate of steak and kidney pudding, peas and chips and a World Cup game between Argentina and Nigeria, on any one of six large TV screens, for under £9.00?

The answer? Only in another Wetherspoons pub.

OK – so they may have a strange payment method where it is cash up front for food but I could live with that. I could only assume that the young folk of Wick are a bit quicker over the ground than the pub management and it was money first, food and beverages second.

Back at June's I was soon settled in my sitting room, nestled in a deep armchair with two bottles of Hobgoblin and the England versus USA game on the TV. I have to say it was a rather pleasant setting to recall the highlights of the day.

My final action was to send a text of condolence to a friend who had just lost the local pub quiz after a tiebreak question. The question was: 'Where do women mostly have curly hair?' He got in first but was embarrassingly wrong and was disqualified – the answer was Africa apparently.

All in all though, the day's events hadn't been too bad – not too bad at all.

The Long Journey Home

AFTER a very pleasant and relaxing Sunday in Wick – a fair percentage of the time being spent in Wetherspoons and the remainder lying on my bed catching up with the papers and World Cup highlights, it was soon Monday and time to board the 08.12 a.m. train from Wick to Inverness on the first stage of my 13-hour journey home.

The four hours run started with me travelling north to Thurso before turning south and 23 further stops before my connection on to Edinburgh.

I have to say that 103 miles in four hours was pretty slow going but why should I care, I was comfortable and warm, my bike was locked safely away and I could sit back and watch the passing scenery without worrying whether my legs would get me up the next hill.

When the line went close to the coast, seals could be seen basking on the sands – it was all rather bewitching. Having said that, staring at a brick wall would have been bewitching after two weeks with my arse in the air and my eyes firmly planted on tarmac roads.

It would have taken a lot to ruffle my feathers on this train ride as I was feeling a touch pleased with myself. I was also going home.

It was fun passing through stations that I had ridden by a few days earlier and I even spotted the exact roads I had taken when moving through Ardgay, Invershin and Lairg. It was a simple pleasure but added to my 'feel good' factor, which was already sky high.

As we slowly edged south I recalled the story that friend Phil Godfrey had told me prior to my trip. Phil, who lives in my home village of Chadlington told me of the time that a train full of crofters and nuclear scientists were on this very same train on their way from Thurso for a day's shopping in Inverness.

Unfortunately the train broke down and the guard informed them that it would be three hours before a replacement would arrive. Making light of the inconvenience, they all disembarked and walked up the line to the nearest hostelry to regroup and drown their disappointment.

Eventually the replacement train arrived and the guard advised the passengers. Unfortunately some of them had imbibed, how can I say this, one too many light refreshments to calm their nerves and were in no mood, or physical condition to leave. After much cajoling by the guard, followed by verbal threats, a mix of crofters and scientists were left to party on, much to the joy of the local publican. The financial loss to the retailers of Inverness was more than made up for by the 'New Years Eve-like' takings of a hotelier in the Highlands on a surprisingly busy Wednesday.

Back on the train the guard was heard to state that it was impossible to tell who were crofters and who were nuclear scientists for the remainder of the journey to Inverness. Wonderful thing alcohol you see – it unites all sections of the community.

Following Phil's story it did cross my mind whether any of them found their way to McCallum's Bar in Union Street?

A lot of people think drink is evil but I prefer to follow the guidance of philosophers far more intelligent than me.

As the great Henry Youngman once said: 'When I read about the evils of drink I immediately gave up reading.'

And Benjamin Franklin, one of the Founding Fathers of the United States who said: 'Beer is proof that God loves us and wants to make us happy.'

Intelligent people with intelligent thoughts.

After what seemed like an age we eventually pulled into Inverness to make the short connection with the train bound for Edinburgh. Here I was very lucky as I was able to find a seat before literally thousands of young people hijacked the train.

They had all been attending the 3rd Highland Rock Ness Festival on the banks of Loch Ness and after a weekend of 'shore-to-shore' din, were heading for home.

I have to be honest and say that I have never heard of 'Friendly Fire', 'Crystal Castle' or 'Soulwax' but I am confident that they are all very fine individuals who play very fine music – as long as the audience is young people under the age of 20.

I just hope that their musical qualities enabled them to be given accommodation a little better than the conditions my fellow passengers had obviously endured, judging by the appearance of them. God they looked a mess.

Some of the females looked no older than 16 or 17 but manfully hauled outsize holdalls on to the racks while at the same time flashing a titillating glimpse of underclothing that I was willing to guarantee hadn't been removed since the three day event commenced the previous Friday. Except for a few very special occasions I suspect.

By all accounts, The Strokes had been a headline act, a fact that confused me slightly as I could not for the life of me understand why a person who sits at the front of the Oxford and Cambridge University boats for their race on the Thames can be of any interest to young people attending rock festivals.

It turned out that I was the stupid one but luckily I was put right by one of the young girls sitting opposite me. They were nothing to do with the Boat Race at all – The Strokes were an American rock band and very good they were too I was told.

Fat Boy Slim and Blondie were two names that I had vaguely heard of but I decided to keep that to myself. I was out of my depth with young girls half a century younger than me so kept quiet and pretended to sleep.

As my fellow passengers gabbled on about the various acts I thought how much a shame it was that Adam Faith and Billy Fury had both gone to that great recording studio in the sky. They would have sent these two stick insects with dresses round their waists wild – stroke or no stroke. Fortunately, Gary Glitter's name never came up.

Two consecutive four-hour stints on trains is a long time especially when the second one is packed solid with sunken eyed, shagged out, rockers so it gave me immense pleasure when I noted that we were passing Murrayfield the home of the Scottish Rugby Union team. We were minutes from Edinburgh.

The girls were also alighting at Waverley Station and it was my intention to assist them with removing their heavy baggage from the overhead rack. Annoyingly it completely slipped my mind until the last bag was down, my only consolation being that I had overseen the whole exercise with my usual visual vigilance.

If the four-hour run from Inverness had given a reasonable impression of sardines packed into a tin, the next ride I embarked on was total luxury by comparison. It was the Virgin cross-country train down to Wolverhampton, a distance of some 280 miles at an average speed of over 76 miles an hour.

The train was less than half full and I was treated to a magnificent ride on the tilting train, again passing through some of the areas I had ridden through on my way north. It was a long time since I had travelled on a true express and in next to no time I had completed three of the four stages of my train journey home.

From Wolverhampton it was only a short hop through Birmingham and on to the NEC International station where Thomas, my youngest son who had ridden with me through Bristol, was waiting to collect me and drive the 50 minutes home.

Fourteen hours after saying goodbye to landlady Jean in Wick I was back in Chadlington, at the end of an adventure that will be recorded in my mind as the most exacting and exciting challenge I had ever undertaken.

It was good to be back in my own home and good to be lying in my own bed after so long away. It was also good to be back with the family.

It wasn't good to know though that I wouldn't be getting a full English breakfast the next morning – it would be back to Fruit 'n Fibre.

Reflections

WHEN an adventure stretches for over 7 months there is much to reflect upon, not just on the short period of the ride but the build-up to it and the wind-down. While the actual time on the road was only a fortnight the entire seven months planning and training programmes , as well as the ride, will also stay in my memory for a long, long time.

There can be no doubt in my mind that meticulous planning made the ride so much easier. While not to everyone's taste, the fact that all the Bed and Breakfast accommodation was booked months in advance not only gave me the inner satisfaction that there was a bed waiting for me at the end of each day, it also gave me the ultimate incentive to hit the daily target I had set myself. In honesty, if I had been making ad hoc overnight arrangements on route I am certain that I would have stopped short of my schedule on more than one occasion.

Typically, of course, I overdid the control by sending packages of Kendal Mint Cake and Jaffa Bars to each B&B. The theory was great and it did mean that I was able to reduce weight, but I am not sure that those two food items were substantially better than anything I could have purchased as I passed through villages. What I do know is that I will never be able to eat Kendal mint and Jaffa cakes again – I'd eaten too many for too long.

From the training angle I think I got that right. The first three months was tedious spending an hour a day on the exercise bike while watching TV but I was fortunate. I was keen and enthusiastic and my weight was visibly reducing – a great motivator.

Riding for a charity was also a key driver, in my case the Derbyshire Children's Holiday Centre. As my sponsors built up there was no turning back from my promise to ride 'End-to-End'. Whether I wanted to or not became irrelevant, I was in and the only way was forward. The thought of letting down the charity and my sponsors got me out of the chair and on to the road on more than one occasion when it was cold and miserable outside.

Record keeping was also an incentive. Every ride whether on the static or road bike was recorded, listing route, mileage, weather conditions, time and weight. Beating previous bests for each route became a priority, another strong motivator to work hard and not just saunter round.

On the exercise bike I recorded calories burned on each ride although I am not altogether convinced of their accuracy. Regardless, it was good to know that somewhere in the region of 800 calories had been burned off when the pudding was being dished out.

Spain was also a great experience even though I only rode for 45 minutes during my two-week stay. Besides fending for myself in a one-eyed kind of way I now know all about the inner workings of the Spanish Health Service and the way eye operations were conducted - with lasers and a cacophony of noise from theatre staff.

Ridiculous as it may sound, the complete isolation I endured for the two weeks I spent there was also excellent grounding for my solo ride.

It was also very exciting to have the privilege of passing Lance Armstrong and his Radio Shack team when I was with my bike coming out of Oliva – a feat that is still awaiting ratification for the Guinness Book of Records. Let's keep the Renault Clio between ourselves, eh?

Finally, and this may seem trivial, my training rides in the Cotswolds allowed me to view one of the prettiest places in the World through different eyes – the eyes of a cyclist. The slower pace, compared to a car, enabled me to enjoy, not endure, the countryside and even now, when taking car journeys I recall trivial things that I saw when riding – memories that never fail to lift my mood.

Contrastingly though, I am also very aware of every pothole within a 30-mile radius of my village – a mini tragedy that exists all over the country. In my view we will never again see quality road surfaces that were the norm only six years ago. In my mind, it's an absolute scandal that road taxes are siphoned off to finance other nonsensical hare-brained schemes while the poor road user is left with third world conditions.

Now – some recollections of my ride.

There can be no doubt that there were some extremely tough days that I had to endure. Don't get me wrong, they were not life- threatening and even in the company of others would have quickly been turned into a good laugh. Hardy, experienced cyclists will also observe, correctly it should be said, that I endured nothing different to what thousands of riders endure on many of their week-end rides. And they would be right.

But remember, I was getting close to 65 years of age, with little knowledge of cycling, and I was travelling alone. It was all a new learning curve for me - crashing heavily in Cornwall, battling through Edinburgh in teeming rain then puncturing, taking on the steep road to the Lecht ski slopes in freezing temperatures in rain and low cloud. They were all fantastic experiences in retrospect, but at the time dismal and dark stages of the ride.

Having said that, I am so pleased that they occurred. Can you imagine, returning from a near 1,100 miles solo ride and my wife asking me about the highlights of the adventure.

'Nothing happened really – what's for dinner?'

Thank goodness it wasn't like that and incidents did occur.

What I have tried to do, is paint a picture of the facts and the feelings I had when times were rough, but sadly I am not equipped to even start to adequately put them into words. What I can say is, that everything written actually happened. I only wish I could have brought each incident to life a fraction more. Life was tough on occasions and there was only one person there to rectify the problems: me.

And, take my word for it, I am a better person for the experience.

The good times are too numerous to mention. The mere fact that an old fart is riding his bike from one end of England to the other end of Scotland is a reason to rejoice in itself. Very few people get the time, opportunity or finance to attempt an adventure of that magnitude in the 'twilight' of their life and I count myself extremely fortunate to have had that chance.

So many events come flooding back when I sit quietly and reminisce, too many to recall here. The sheer joy of travelling through the beautiful lanes of Great Britain on a warm sunny day makes one realise just how fortunate we are to live in a country like ours.

Conversely it is frightening to contemplate how commercialised our lives have become. Television, wall-to-wall with reality shows, computers with Facebook and Twitter, game boys and Wi-Fi may all be progress of a fashion but they block out the simple pleasures of walking, riding, climbing and playing sports especially in a child's formative years.

My time on the road reminded me of the simple pleasures of life.

How can I describe riding along beautiful Cornish lanes on a cloudless day in late May – unleashed from seven months of dedicated training? I can't – it's just an unbelievable sense of freedom. Go to Marazion and look out into the bay to St Michael's Mount – is there a better backdrop to enjoy on the first day?

How can I explain shedding tears of joy as I cycled between South Molton and Taunton on my third day on the road? I can't and won't even try to – all I know is that it was a good place to be at that moment and I am not ashamed or embarrassed to admit it.

How can I tell you of my true feelings when riding over the Trough Of Bowland in Lancashire with John and Frances Barr, the couple that had ridden up from the Pyrenees? It is impossible. The natural rugged beauty all around, the respect I had for a couple who loved cycling and accepted the highs and lows as part of life are all very personal to me and will never be forgotten.

And, how do I even begin to convey my feelings on the natural tranquillity and raw landscape around the Crask Inn in Sutherland? The harsh, but so satisfyingly simple lives led by Mike and Kai Geldred? It's not a lifestyle for me and probably not for you either, but it is an education to see it for real. They are so happy in that environment and I respect them for it.

The recollections of my LEJOG ride will never leave me, neither will my memories and feelings I have for the people I met as I rode through Britain. Many have been mentioned already, but special reference should be made to the many landladies and landlords of the Bed and Breakfasts I stayed in. I had never set foot in a B&B until my ride but I will do so again and most certainly in preference to 5-star hotels.

With only two exceptions they were totally brilliant, washing my cycling gear, providing taxi services to pubs and restaurants, never failing to provide spotless accommodation and fabulous breakfasts. On one occasion I was even taken shopping, on another invited to sit in their private sitting room watching the Eurovision Song Contest while drinking their wine. Why, in Grantown-on-Spey I even wore a pair of the landlord's trainers to the pub. Their kindness and warmth won't be forgotten.

Tell me where a 5-star hotel offers any of that quality, 'I really care' service for around £30.00 a night?

And, not to mention of course the characters that I have endeavoured to bring to life. From Anne in Cheddar who loved to tell a tale, to race-horse owner Jack in the Forest of Dean, Wing Commander Mike Purdie in Glenshee who paid me to stay with him, and Jean in Wick who was so much fun. Characters, all of them, who made my trip the pleasurable experience it was.

And that is before I recall the Indian coffee shop owner in Tintagel, the outsize ladies of Hanham, Bristol, the Goliath who managed the garage in Herefordshire and the 'Russian immigrant' I met on the Forth Bridge. There are just too many to mention but they all played a part in making my adventure one of the best times of my life.

The family have also been great. Can you think what it must be like to live with someone who, for over seven months, is totally obsessed and single-minded about riding a bike around a few lanes for a couple of weeks. Christine, my wife and children Daniel, James, Charlotte and Thomas should all receive plaudits for their patience and understanding – I must have been the biggest bore in the world leading up to the event. As I now tell them: 'At least I had an excuse to be boring, I haven't now.'

Another happy memory is of all the encouraging and motivating texts and calls I received from family and friends while on my journey. It really made my day when my mobile phone alerted me that someone was in contact. Sounds bloody stupid to say it now but at the time it kept my chin up and was really appreciated.

My final reflection is to the sponsors and the Derbyshire Children's Holiday Centre charity that I rode for. So many people have dug deeply into their pockets to support the cause of providing holidays for underprivileged children and it was a tremendously proud moment when I was able to present a cheque for £5,500 to Bill Tomlinson, head of the charity, at Pride Park Derby before a Rams home game.

Now all I have is a photo album and a few thousand words, but they don't come anywhere close to capturing the great moments I had. What I do have though, are countless memories that will never be erased.

Who would have thought it possible that a retired, overweight, unfit man, who hadn't ridden a bike for 50 years, would suddenly decide to get off his backside, lose three unwanted stones, then take on the might of the classic Land's End to John O'Groats 'End-to-End' cycle ride?

I thought it possible and did just that – to prove to myself that anything can be done with the right inspiration, desire and discipline. I did it primarily for me, to convince myself that there was still life in me. I did it to prove that if I wanted something badly enough and was prepared to work hard I could have it. All it would take was discipline and desire.

Most of all, I rode Land's End to John O'Groats as an example to my children. Hopefully as they work their way through their lives they will identify targets and personal goals and go after them with the same enthusiasm and single-mindedness that I was fortunate enough to possess.

I chased a dream and gave it 100 per cent – and following the realisation of that dream was able look in the mirror and be proud of the face that was looking back at me.

All that is needed is effort and a never-say-die spirit.

Nobody can argue with that legacy.

About the Author

Nigel Cleevely was born in Cheltenham on 23 December 1945. While at Cheltenham Grammar School he represented Gloucestershire at Cricket and Rugby Union. He also played Football for his county at youth level, before joining Derby County as a professional footballer.

He scored on his debut against Charlton Athletic when just 18 years of age, but after four seasons with the club County's Manager, Brian Clough, moved him on to Burton Albion.

During his business career he held senior positions with British Midland Airways, Clarksons Holidays and finally Thomson Travel where he served as Operations Director responsible for over 800 Holiday shops.

After retiring at the age of 54 he undertook consultancy work with Sandals and Beaches Resorts, an all inclusive luxury holiday group with hotels throughout the Caribbean.

His leisure activities include running numerous marathons, walking the Cotswold and Pennine Ways, as well as scaling the UK mainland's three major peaks, Snowdon, Scafell and Ben Nevis in less than 30 hours.

He now lives in a small village in the Cotswolds with his wife, Christine. He has four children, Daniel, James, Charlotte and Thomas and five grandchildren.

Training Log and Statistics

November 2009							
Date	**Bike Type**	**Time**		**Distance**	**Calories/Weather**	**Weight**	
		hrs	mins	miles	Kcal	st	lbs
Sun 1st	Static	1	00	17.0	750	14	10
Mon 2nd	Static	0	45	14.0	54	14	10
Tues 3rd	Static	1	05	18.3	800	14	9
Wed 4th	Road	1	30	17.7	Cold, Breezy	14	9
Fri 6th	Road	1	30	17.0	Overcast	14	8
Sun 8th	Static	1	10	20.2	812	14	7
Tues 10th	Static	1	05	18.3	850	14	7
Wed 11th	Static	0	45	14.0	650	14	6
Thur 12th	Road	1	30	17.7	Overcast	14	5
Fri 13th	Static	0	35	11.1	515	14	4
Sun 15th	Static	1	00	17.9	836	14	4
Tues 17th	Static	1	00	17.2	500	14	3
Thur 19th	Static	1	00	17.7	820	14	2
Sat 21st	Static	1	00	18.0	839	14	2
Sun 22nd	Static	1	00	18.0	838	14	1
Wed 25th	Static	1	00	18.4	850	14	1
Thur 26th	Static	1	00	18.4	950	14	0
Fri 27th	Static	1	00	18.2	845	14	0
Sat 28th	Static	1	00	17.8	845	13	12
Mon 30th	Static	1	00	17.8	824	13	11

December 2009

Date	Bike Type	Time		Distance	Calories/Weather	Weight	
		hrs	mins	miles	Kcal	st	lbs
Tues 1st	Static	1	00	18.3	848	13	11
Wed 2nd	Static	1	00	18.4	854	13	11
Mon 7th	Static	1	00	17.8	825	13	11
Tues 8th	Static	1	00	18.6	860	13	11
Wed 9th	Static	1	00	18.1	865	13	9
Thurs 10th	Road	1	28	17.7	Cold, dry, sunny	13	8
Fri 11th	Static	1	00	17.6	815	13	7
Sun 13th	Static	1	00	18.5	857	13	10
Mon 14th	Static	1	00	18.1	843	13	9
Tues 15th	Static	1	00	18.5	858	13	9
Thurs 17th	Static	1	00	18.8	861	13	8
Fri 18th	Static	1	00	18.4	852	13	8
Sat 19th	Static	1	00	18.2	847	13	8
Mon 21st	Static	1	00	18.8	867	13	7
Tues 22nd	Static	1	00	17.8	823	13	5
Wed 23rd	Static	1	00	18.4	849	13	5
Thurs 24th	Static	1	00	18.2	846	13	5
Fri 25th	Static	1	00	18.1	841	13	7
Sun 27th	Static	1	00	18.5	854	13	9
Mon 28th	Static	1	00	18.4	850	13	7
Wed 30th	Static	1	00	18.8	872	13	7
Thurs 31st	Static	1	00	18.4	850	13	8
Total		22	28	402.4		- 0	3

Date	Bike Type	Time		Distance	Calories/Weather	Weight	
		hrs	mins	miles	Kcal	st	lbs
Fri 1st	Static	1	00	18.2	847	13	10
Sat 2nd	Static	1	00	17.8	825	13	8
Mon 4th	Static	1	00	18.3	849	13	8
Tues 5th	Static	1	00	18.7	863	13	6
Wed 6th	Static	1	00	18.6	860	13	6
Thurs 7th	Static	1	00	18.3	848	13	6
Fri 8th	Static	1	00	18.3	848	13	6
Sun 10th	Static	1	00	18.4	851	13	6
Tues 12th	Static	1	12	21.6	1000	13	7
Wed 13th	Static	1	00	18.1	842	13	5
Thurs 14th	Static	1	00	18.2	846	13	5
Fri 15th	Static	1	00	18.0	830	13	5
Sat 16th	Static	1	00	18.3	845	13	6
Mon 18th	Static	1	00	18.4	852	13	8
Tues 19th	Static	1	00	18.3	848	13	7
Wed 20th	Static	1	00	18.2	845	13	5
Thurs 21st	Static	1	00	18.2	846	13	5
Fri 22nd	Static	1	00	18.1	843	13	5
Sun 24th	Static	1	00	18.2	846	13	4
Mon 25th	Static	1	00	18.7	867	13	4
Tues 26th	Static	1	00	18.4	849	13	4
Wed 27th	Static	1	00	17.8	911	13	3
Thurs 28th	Static	1	00	18.1	841	13	2
Total		23	12	423.2		- 0	8

Date	Bike Type	Time		Distance	Calories/Weather	Weight	
February 2010							
		hrs	mins	miles	Kcal	st	lbs
Wed 10th	Spain	0	45	10.0	sun,breezy	No record	
Sat 13th	Static	1	00	18.3	845	13	3
Sun 14th	Road	1	26	17.7	Cold, dry, breezy	No record	
Mon 15th	Road	2	42	31.2	Cold, drizzle	13	1
Tues 16th	Static	1	00	17.4	806	13	1
Wed 17th	Static	1	00	17.6	815	13	2
Thurs 18th	Static	1	00	18.3	849	13	0
Fri 19th	Static	1	00	18.3	848	13	1
Sat 20th	Road	4	52	50.5	Sunny, cold	13	1
Mon 22nd	Static	1	00	17.7	823	13	1
Tues 23rd	Static	1	00	17.6	815	13	0
Wed 24th	Road	2	10	25.0	Dry, overcast	13	0
Thurs 25th	Road	1	42	18.0	Cold, drizzle	13	0
Fri 26th	Static	0	40	12.3	570	12	12
Sat 27th	Static	1	00	18.1	843	12	13
Sun 28th	Static	1	00	17.1	819	12	13
Total		21	57	325.1		- 0	4

March 2010

Date	Bike Type	Time		Distance	Calories/Weather	Weight	
		hrs	mins	miles	Kcal	st	lbs
Mon 1st	Road	2	13	26.0	Cold,sunny	12	12
Tues 2nd	Road	1	32	18.0	Cold, sunny	12	12
Wed 3rd	Road	1	35	18.0	Cold, cloudy	12	11
Sat 6th	Static	1	00	17.6	816	12	12
Sun 7th	Road	4	00	46.0	Cold, sunny	12	11
Mon 8th	Road	1	29	17.7	Cold, sunny	12	11
Tues 9th	Static	1	00	18.1	841	12	11
Wed 10th	Road	2	51	32.6	Cold, breezy	12	10
Thurs 11th	Static	1	00	18.1	844	12	9
Fri 12th	Static	1	00	18.2	846	12	10
Sat 13th	Road	0	48	10.1	Cold, sunny	12	10
Mon 15th	Road	3	10	34.0	Sunny, blustery	12	11
Tues 16th	Road	1	24	17.0	Sunny,breezy	12	9
Wed 17th	Road	3	30	42.0	Cloudy, dry	12	8
Thurs 18th	Road	2	15	26.9	Warm, breezy	12	8
Fri 19th	Static	1	00	17.5	929	12	9
Mon 22nd	Road	2	35	30.5	Overcast, showers	12	10
Tues 23rd	Road	1	20	17.0	Cool, breezy	12	9
Wed 24th	Road	1	45	22.7	Dry,warm	12	8
Thurs 25th	Road	1	45	23.0	Rain	12	8
Fri 26th	Road	2	10	26.0	Breezy,showers	12	8
Sat 27th	Road	3	30	40.2	Cool, breezy	12	8
Mon 29th	Road	1	58	23.4	Showery,slight breeze	12	9
Tues 30th	Static	1	00	17.6	814	12	8
Wed 31st	Static	1	00	17.5	811	12	8
Total		51	33	595.7		- 0	4

April 2010

Date	Bike Type	Time		Distance	Calories/Weather	Weight	
		hrs	mins	miles	Kcal	st	lbs
Thurs 1st	Road	2	04	25.2	Cold, breezy	12	7
Fri 2nd	Road	2	00	24.0	Dry, slight breeze	12	7
Sat 3rd	Static	0	30	8.7	402	12	8
Sun 4th	Road	3	27	41.9	Sunny, Cool breeze	12	8
Mon 5th	Road	1	26	17.7	Sunny, windy	12	7
Wed 7th	Road	2	07	25.0	Dry, breezy	12	9
Thurs 8th	Road	2	20	32.0	Sunny, warm	12	7
Fri 9th	Road	1	42	21.0	Sunny, warm	12	6
Sun 11th	Road	5	08	68.0	Cool, breezy	12	7
Mon 12th	Road	1	35	20.0	Cool, breezy	12	7
Tues 13th	Road	2	00	25.0	Sun, breezy	12	7
Thurs 15th	Road	2	38	32.6	Cloudy, slight breeze	12	7
Fri 16th	Road	1	48	27.7	Sun, stiff breeze	12	6
Sat 17th	Road	1	45	23.4	Sunny, calm	12	6
Sun 18th	Road	4	12	52.8	Sunny, slight breeze	12	5
Mon 19th	Road	1	20	17.7	Sunny, breezy	12	4
Tues 20th	Road	1	53	24.0	Sunny, breezy	12	3
Thurs 22nd	Road	2	00	26.6	Sunny, cool	12	5
Fri 23rd	Road	2	05	27.3	Sunny, warm	12	4
Sat 24th	Road	2	02	25.0	Sunny, breezy	12	4
Sun 25th	Road	3	52	51.1	Coudy, breezy	12	4
Mon 26th	Road	0	55	12.0	Cloudy, breezy	12	4
Tues 27th	Road	2	29	31.3	Sunny, breezy	12	4
Thurs 29th	Road	1	46	24.0	Calm, drizzle	12	4
Fri 30th	Road	1	43	21.0	Sun, Strong breeze	12	3
Total		56	45	706.0		- 0	4

May 2010

Date	Bike Type	Time		Distance	Calories/Weather	Weight	
		hrs	mins	miles	Kcal	st	lbs
Sat 1st	Road	3	57	52.4	Cool, dry	12	2
Sun 2nd	Static	1	00	18.5	825	12	2
Mon 3rd	Road	1	47	23.1	Overcast, cold, windy	12	2
Tues 4th	Road	2	02	25.2	Sunny, breezy	12	2
Wed 5th	Road	1	08	15.0	Cloudy	12	1
Thurs 6th	Road	2	35	31.3	Cool, breezy	12	2
Fri 7th	Road	1	44	21.0	Strong breeze	12	1
Sun 9th	Road	1	58	24.0	Cool, breezy	12	2
Sun 9th	Road	1	55	23.7	Cool, breezy	12	2
Mon 10th	Road	0	40	10.1	sunny, breezy	12	2
Tues 11th	Road	1	45	22.2	Sun, cool breeze	12	2
Wed 12th	Road	2	25	31.3	Overcast, breezy	12	2
Thurs 13th	Road	1	16	17.7	Warm, slight breeze	12	1
Fri 14th	Road	1	42	23.1	Overcast, breezy	12	1
Sun 16th	Road	4	06	51.3	Sun, slight breeze	12	2
Mon 17th	Road	1	23	17.7	Sun. Warm	12	0
Tues 18th	Road	1	51	23.7	Sun, warm	12	1
Wed 19th	Road	2	09	26.4	Sun, slight breeze	12	1
Thurs 20th	Road	1	45	23.7	Sun, slight breeze	12	1
Sat 22nd	Road	1	36	21.0	Sun, slight breeze	12	2
Sun 23rd	Road	2	57	37.1	Hot, warm breeze	12	2
Mon 24th	Road	1	24	17.7	Warm, slight breeze	12	2
Tues 25th	Road	1	10	14.3	Cool, breezy	12	1
Total		47	42	571.3		- 0	1